PIERRE VIRET
THE THEOLOGIAN

REFORMATION THEOLOGY AND
CONTEMPORARY APPLICATION

BOOKS BY JEAN-MARC BERTHOUD

Pierre Viret: the Forgotten Giant of the Reformation

In Defense of God's Law (forthcoming)

Calvin et la France

Création Bible et Science

Des Acts de l'Église: le Christianisme en Suisse romande

L'alliance de Dieu à travers l'Écriture sainte: une théologie biblique

L'école et la famille contre l'utopie

*L'Église au pied du mur. Le diagnostic
toujours actuel du Prophète Ésaïe*

*Le Huitième Commandement:
L'Économie, le Vol et l'Ordre de la Création*

Le règne terrestre de Dieu: Politique, Nations et Foi chrétienne

L'Histoire Alliancielle de l'Église dans le Monde

Une religion sans Dieu: les droits de l'Homme contre l'Évangile

PIERRE VIRET
THE THEOLOGIAN

REFORMATION THEOLOGY AND
CONTEMPORARY APPLICATION

by Jean-Marc Berthoud

Translated by R. A. Sheats

Psalm 78 Ministries

www.psalm78ministries.com

Pierre Viret the Theologian: Reformation Theology and Contemporary Application

by Jean-Marc Berthoud

Translated by R. A. Sheats

Copyright © 2019 Psalm 78 Ministries

All rights reserved.
No part of this publication may be reproduced or distributed in any form or by any means, without written consent from the publisher.

Published by:

Psalm 78 Ministries
P. O. Box 950
Monticello, FL 32345

psalm78ministries.com

ISBN: 978-1-070261652

Biblical quotations are taken from the King James Version of the Holy Scriptures.

TABLE OF CONTENTS

Translator's Note 7

1 Pierre Viret and the Church's Refusal
   to Fold before the Power of the State 9

2 Pierre Viret and the Knowledge of God 29

3 Understanding the Created World and History 57

4 Assessing Viret's Theology:
   John Calvin in the light of Pierre Viret 65

5 Man as the Image of God according to Pierre Viret:
   A Reading by Douglas Kelly 75

6 Pierre Viret and Natural Law 95

7 Natural Law Applied: the Diversity of Laws
   and the Modern Abuse of Natural Law 111

8 A Call to Return to the Divinely-created Natural Order . . 127

9 Viret and the Application of God's Law to Society 133

APPENDIX

1 Pierre Viret, Herald of Conceptual Realism in Science:
   The physical, biological, theological, and moral science
   of a universe created, ordered, and sustained by God . . . 145

2 The True Issue of the Debate between Science and Faith . . . 149

TRANSLATED WORKS OF PIERRE VIRET

The Catechism of Pierre Viret

The Christian and the Magistrate

Defend the Truth: a Conversation on the Ninth Commandment

His Glorious Bride: A Practical Look at Jesus Christ's Church

Honor thy Father and Mother

Jesus Christ: the Believer's Comfort and Joy

Letters of Comfort to the Persecuted Church

Marvelous Trinity: the Believer's Hope and Delight

No Other God: A Practical Look at a Personal God

Nothing Like God: A Penetrating Application of the Second Commandment

Remember the Sabbath Day

Simple Exposition of the Christian Faith

Taking His Name in Vain

Thou Shalt Not Commit Adultery

Thou Shalt Not Covet

Thou Shalt Not Kill: A Plea for Life

Thou Shalt Not Steal

Translator's Note

The text of this book has been drawn from the second volume of Jean-Marc Berthoud's five volume set, *L'Histoire alliancielle de l'Église dans le Monde: L'aboutissement Thomiste, l'automne du Moyen Age, le renouveau de la Réforme* (2017), pages 494-605. Chapter nine of *Pierre Viret the Theologian* has been adapted from a lecture given at I Congresso Internacional, *Reforma Protestante y Libertades en Europa*, Facultad de Communicaciòn, University of Sevilla, Spain on March 31, 2009.

It is my hope that the present translation will offer an English-speaking audience easy access to the clarity and precision of Jean-Marc Berthoud's writings on the life and theology of Pierre Viret, the Swiss Reformer known as *the Angel of the Reformation*. Within this work the author addresses both Viret's writings and their theological and philosophical implications while providing poignantly relevant applications to the contemporary moral battles of our own day.

I would like to express my debt of gratitude to Jean-Marc for looking over and correcting my translation of this work and for the insightful comments and adjustments he has offered along the way. May this small work be useful in the Church's ongoing work of *semper reformanda*.

CHAPTER ONE

Pierre Viret and the Church's Refusal to Fold before the Power of the State

Twas the night before Christmas, 1558. In the vicarage of the Madeleine, at the foot of the cathedral in Lausanne (present-day Switzerland), Sebastienne Viret anxiously and with some impatience awaited the return of her husband, who for some time had been detained by the debates of the local Council of the Two Hundred.

What could these men be discussing so late into the night on Christmas Eve? It was a question concerning the postponement of the celebration of the Lord's Supper, held three times a year—at Passover, Pentecost, and Christmas. An eight-day postponement of the supper had been requested, moving the celebration back to the first of the New Year. This earnest request came from the three pastors of the cathedral: Pierre Viret, Jacques Valier, and Armand Banc, who desired this delay in order to be able to arrange the time necessary for the Consistory to conduct an examination—though not implement any discipline—of those whom the pastors considered unworthy to partake of the Supper because of their scandalous life or faltering faith. They sought at all costs to quickly make the most of the last concession of the Bernese lords.

We find here the culminating point of a conflict of powers between the pastors of the *Classe* of Lausanne (an assembly of pastors and deacons of the region spanning from Lausanne to Vevey) on the one hand—of whom Pierre Viret was the undisputed leader—who called for the right of the Consistory (that is, of the church's officers and, through them, of the church itself) to excommunicate unbelievers; and, on the other hand, the political authority of the Pays de Vaud, Their Excellencies of Bern, who loathed to hear the least whisper of the smallest departure from the absolute control they exercised over their Vaudois subjects.

After a turbulent debate, the Lausanne Council acceded to the demands of the pastors. The celebration of the Lord's Supper would be postponed a single week.

But what now would the Council and the Senate of Bern do? For, since the conquest of 1536, the power of the Pays de Vaud had rested in their hands. What would be the reaction of those who were called by their subjects: *Our Illustrious, High, Powerful, and Sovereign Lords, their Excellencies of the City and Republic of Bern?*

The response was not long in coming. Informed the same day by their bailiff, the lords of Bern responded with the greatest vigor. The celebration of the Lord's Supper on the first day of the year was quite simply banned and a delegation from the Senate was immediately sent to Lausanne with rigorous instructions: Viret and his two colleagues were to be dismissed from their offices, effective immediately. The City Council received a strong reprimand for their "abuse of power," and the *Classe* of Lausanne received orders to fill the pastoral posts which had thus been made vacant. The *Classe's* unanimous refusal to replace Viret and his colleagues brought about the imprisonment of all its members.

Released after three days, these pastors were summoned to appear before the Senate at Bern on February 23-25, 1559. They were then given the alternative: submit unconditionally to the "Reformation of Their Excellencies of Bern" or resign from their office. About thirty of the pastors chose exile, among whom were nearly all the professors of the flourishing Academy founded by Viret and Their Excellencies of Bern in 1537. The dean of the Academy, the famous Theodore Beza who had arrived in Lausanne in 1549, had realized earlier than his colleagues the futility of continuing the battle with the Bernese power for the spiritual independence of the Vaudois Church. In August of 1558 he had requested leave and rejoined Calvin in Geneva. He there assisted in founding the famous Theological Academy which employed those exiled from the Lausanne Academy to engage in the work of spreading the Reformation throughout the entirety of Europe. At the end of February 1559, Pierre Viret, finally seeing that nothing more could be obtained, rejoined his friends Calvin and Beza at Geneva, where he shortly afterward received the sentence of perpetual banishment pronounced against him by the Bernese authorities.

Thus, at the age of 48, after a fruitful ministry of twenty-eight years, Pierre Viret left his homeland forever, to which he would later write, "If I should wish that God be glorified among men, where should I desire that He be so more than in the country of my birth?"[1]

Who then was this man, so little inclined to conflicts and controversies, who thus provoked such a violent tempest among these Vaudois, a tempest to which we can scarcely find an equal before the great schism of 1847? Who was this Pierre Viret, this Swiss Reformer, a friend and fellow-soldier of William Farel, John Calvin, and Theodore Beza, the faithful pastor who was called *the Angel of the Reformation?*[2] Drug into innumerable combats in order to establish a true Reformation in the Pays de Vaud, he was forced to engage in a war of almost twenty years with his overlords in an effort to obtain true spiritual autonomy for the Church in the face of the pretensions of the absolute sovereignty of the Bernese state. This church leader capable of such a persistent long-term fight could in all sincerity write of himself:

> I have always naturally loved peace and have always held all dissentions and troubles in horror. However, the knowledge it pleased God to give me of His Word from my youth and the experience I have gained from

---

[1] Pierre Viret, *De vrai ministère de la vraie église de Jésus-Christ* (Geneva, 1560). These words appear on the monument erected in his honor on Pierre Viret Street at the foot of the Lausanne Cathedral.

[2] On Pierre Viret, see the following biographies: R. A. Sheats, *Pierre Viret: the Angel of the Reformation* (Zurich Publishing, Tallahassee, FL, 2012), and Jean-Marc Berthoud, *Pierre Viret: A Forgotten Giant of the Reformation* (Zurich Publishing, 2010).

> the exercise of the ministry of His holy Gospel incites me still more to push for peace and concord and to consider even more diligently what Jesus Christ said, "Blessed are the peacemakers, for they shall be called the children of God."[3]

On August 1, 1550, at a time when he was pressed with the inextricable difficulties occasioned by Bern's obstinate desire to retain supreme control over the Church, Viret wrote to his friend Calvin:

> One thing comforts me, which is the peace which reigns in my house, the mutual affection and the goodwill among ministers and professors, and the constant progress of our schools. If these things were lacking, I could not live here, but would be constrained to depart.[4]

Pierre Viret was born—according to the traditional date[5]—in 1511 in the ancient Roman and Burgundian small town of Orbe, of particularly pious middle-class parents. His father was a tailor by profession. After a primary education in the parish school of Orbe—which one could scarcely call mediocre considering Viret's remarkable knowledge, immense education, and perfect mastery of ancient languages, particularly Latin—he left his native village at the end of 1527 at the age of seventeen in order to complete his studies at Paris, where he intended to prepare himself for the priesthood. At Paris he entered the College Montaigu, which had been frequented before him by John Calvin and where he had as a classmate Ignatius of Loyola, the founder of the Jesuits. Like Calvin, he was strongly marked by the Scottish philosophical teaching of the Scotist-leaning

---

[3] Huguette Chausson, *Pierre Viret: Ce Viret que fit virer* (Eglise Nationale Vaudoise, Lausanne, 1961), p. 63.

[4] Henri Vuilleumier, *Histoire de l'Église Réformée du Pays de Vaud, Tome I* (Editions La Concorde, Lausanne, 1927), page 425.

[5] Recent research fixes Viret's birth two years earlier, in 1509, making him the same age as his fellow-laborer and friend John Calvin.

John Major.⁶ This common influence in part explains the close resemblance of the thought of the two Reformers.

At Paris, after bitter spiritual battles, Pierre Viret was converted to the Evangelical faith and opted for the *Lutheranism* which at that time could so easily conduct those who accepted it to the pyres kindled by the false church. He knew the anguish of those "poor consciences," as he described himself, "so troubled and nearly desperate, not knowing which way to turn."⁷ He added: "At a young age, being still at school, the goodness of God withdrew me from that labyrinth of error before I was plunged too deeply into that Babylon."⁸

This Babylon was, obviously, the Roman Church. In the beginning of 1531 we find Viret at Orbe, having fled the capital in order to escape from the persecution which again ruthlessly held sway over those who dared to profess Evangelical convictions.

From the beginning of 1528, after the famous Disputation of Bern in which (among others) Ulrich Zwingli, Martin Bucer, Wolfgang Capito, Johannes Oecolampadius, and William Farel participated, Their Excellencies of Bern embraced the Reformation they advocated. The Great Order of the Reformation of February 7, 1528 established the Word of God as the sole foundation of the Church in all territories under Bernese authority.

At the close of the Burgundian wars at the end of the fifteenth century, the Bernese jointly held in common with their fellow-Swiss canton Fribourg a certain number of *baillages:* Orbe, Echallens, Morat, Grandson, Avenches, Payerne, etc. Wherever this was the case, Their Excellencies sought to advance both the Reformed Faith as well as their own territorial extension. They certainly acted with religious conviction, but we can't doubt that they were also moved by seriously thought-out long-term goals of political conquest.

Thus William Farel, furnished with a diplomatic mandate officially issued by the Bernese authorities, preached the Word of

---

⁶ Thomas F. Torrance, *The Hermeneutics of John Calvin* (Scottish Academic Press, Edinburgh, 1987). See pages 23-57: "John Major of Haddington."
⁷ Jean Barnaud, *Pierre Viret, Sa Vie et Son Oeuvre* (Saint-Amans, 1911), p. 24.
⁸ Henri Vuilleumier, *Notre Pierre Viret* (Librairie Payot & Cie, Lausanne, 1911), p. 15.

God in all the common *baillages*. Wherever he went his presence provoked many disorders and disputes but, by the grace of God, his work also met with numerous conversions. As an ambassador of God, he was also provided with letters of recommendation from the Bernese authorities which made him their delegate, the diplomatic agent of Their Excellencies. Thus, in the first years of his activity in French-speaking Switzerland, Farel was both the iron lance of the Gospel as well as the political expansionist of Bern.

For Bern had adopted the Zwinglian reform in which the political authority, after having dismantled the remains of a defective ecclesiastical authority, entirely absorbed it to its own advantage. Bern was an example not of a State Church in which the Church, joined to the State, would at the same time be preserved as an independent spiritual reality, but rather a true State-Church. The Caesaro-papism of the Roman Church was replaced by the religious autocracy of a unified Christian State in which all real distinction between temporal and spiritual powers had the tendency to disappear. On both sides the distinction—not the opposition!—which the Bible established between the spiritual power (the Church wielding the sword of the Spirit, the Word of God) and the temporal power (the State wielding the sword) was lost. This confusion of powers certainly explains both the pyres of the Roman Church as well as the drowning of the pacifist Christian Mennonite Baptists in the Limmatt at Zurich by Zwingli's State-Church.[9] The death of Zwingli, sword in hand, at Kappel on October 11, 1531 was the logical consequence of such a confusion of the temporal with the spiritual.

Bern had adopted the Zwinglian vision of a State-Church in which the magistrates dominated the ecclesiastical power with a high hand. Until the eighteenth century, Their Excellencies also arrested the Baptists who dared to enter their territory and sold them at the slave market of Venice to the Turks, who sent them to man their galleys. Georges de Lagarde put his finger—

---

[9] An indispensable work on this subject is that by John Horsch, *Mennonites in Europe* (Mennonite Publishing House, Scottsdale, PA, 1971 [1942]).

certainly rather heavily—on the absolutist and statist tendencies of the Zwinglian reform when he wrote:

> The Zurich State achieved within its breast the unity of public life. It was solely responsible before God for all acts, whether political or religious. As both high priest and king, it revived the attributes of the ancient pagan cities. It was sovereign.[10]

Later, under the prudent and courageous direction of Heinrich Bullinger, the church of Zurich recovered a part of its spiritual autonomy in relation to the State. Bern was the Swiss city which pushed the hardest to found the Zwinglian position. As James Good, the American historian of the Reformed Churches in Switzerland, wrote:

> For nowhere were Zwingli's Erastian views of the relations of Church and state so fully developed as in Bern, where not only were church and state united, but the Church was merely an arm of the state. In giving up the rule by bishops in the Reformation, the state had taken the bishop's place and ruled with his authority.[11]

Gonzague de Reynold, in his study on the spirit of Bern, helps us better understand to what extent this vision of the relationships between the State and the Church agreed with the secular politics of Their Excellencies:

> For Bern, from its inception, is the only political entity within the Confederation of Swiss cantons which possesses a State strategy . . . a political vision that extends to its natural limits, from the summits of the

---

[10] Georges de Lagarde, *Recherches sur l'esprit politique de la Réforme* (Picard, Paris, 1926), p. 312. In the collegiate church of St. Vincent in Bern, below the chancel, where a symbol of the divinity is generally found in the archway, we find instead the bear, the heraldic symbol of the Republic of Bern.

[11] James I. Good, *History of the Swiss Reformed Church since the Reformation* (Sunday School Board, Philadelphia, 1913), p. 41.

Alps and the crest of the Jura. . . . A political realism, unhampered by theories, and indeed often devoid of scruples; its politics being hostile to doctrines and suspicious of ideas. . . . To be its own master and to reign over others. To brook no superior power; consequently, to subordinate the Church to the State and education to politics.[12]

We're not dealing here with the spirit of the Bernese people but with that of the political elite who ruled throughout the entire medieval and patrician epoch. Gonzague de Reynold, speaking even more clearly of the political spirit of Bern, says:

The final, most pronounced characteristic of this spirit is a jealousy of authority.
I will analyze it.
Not even the slightest amount of power must be allowed to escape, to slip through the cracks; it must be retained, to the very last particle; it must be asserted and rendered absolute.
Power must be limited to the ancient *bourgeois,* then only to the patrician families.
An attentiveness must be maintained to ensure that no faction, no personal ambition might seize it; every family must be forbidden from having more than one representative in the Senate and more than a hundred thousand *livres* in its purse.
The discussion of power must be forbidden—even speaking well of it cannot be permitted; silence must be exercised, with lips sealed; it must be withdrawn from spectators, curious, and strangers.
Favor must often be given, sometimes to reforms, but never to concessions.
Respect of power must be demanded as a sacred thing, given by God.[13]

---

[12] Gonzague de Reynold, *Le Génie de Berne et l'Ame de Fribourg* (Payot, Lausanne, 1934 [1929]), pp. 52-53.
[13] Gonzague de Reynold, *Raconte la Suisse et son histoire* (Payot, Lausanne, 1965), p. 119.

We here find ourselves, to some extent, witnessing a resurrection of the spirit which animated the Republic—and then the Empire—of Rome, a heritage which the leaders of the Republic of Bern were well aware of. Gonzague de Reynold writes:

> This ancient city, powerful and poor of a former time, the humanists were pleased to compare to Sparta; the now-powerful Republic equated herself with Rome as she engraved in stone the four sacred letters: S.P.Q.B.: *Senatus Populusque Bernensis*.[14]

This is the power that God in His providence used to back up William Farel in his efforts to uproot the errors of papal Rome within French-speaking Switzerland.

On Palm Sunday of 1531 Farel was in Orbe, equipped with an order from Their Excellencies to preach the Word of God at all costs. This is not the place to describe the battles which followed and the way in which the town was little by little won to the Gospel. Among the listeners of the fiery Dauphine evangelist was found a young man of twenty years, in full agreement with his preaching. This was our Pierre Viret, and Farel quickly detected in him the graces of God, despite his modesty and young age. As he was later to do with Calvin, Farel imposed the calling of a minister of the Word of God upon Viret and established him as pastor of the nascent community. Viret had the joy of bringing his father and mother to the knowledge of salvation, and when he left Orbe fifteen months later he left a flourishing congregation. From ten people it had increased to more than eighty.

In 1534, after an itinerant ministry during which he received a sword wound in the back—a forceful argument from a monk of the Payerne Abbey—we find Viret at Farel's side in Geneva. There again an attempt was made on his life, this time by poison. He survived, though his health was never fully restored.

In 1536, after a short journey to Germany to implore aid in favor of the Vaudois of Piedmont who were being harshly persecuted by Charles II of Savoy and Francis I of France, Viret

---

[14] Gonzague de Reynold, *Le Génie de Berne*, p. 32.

settled in Lausanne, where he began to preach the Gospel even before the arrival of the Bernese troops. The same year saw the conquest of the Pays de Vaud by Bern and Fribourg as well as the famous Lausanne Disputation in which Viret—though he was no more than twenty-five—took the lead role alongside Farel. Following this disputation came the Bernese proclamation of the Reformation Edicts which imposed the Reformation by force on a population still largely established in the old Catholic traditions. Apart from the period stretching from January 1541 to July 1542 when he assisted Calvin at Geneva, Viret, until his exile in 1559, consecrated all his energies and the great gifts which God had given him to feed the Vaudois church, particularly his Lausanne parishioners.

This long pastoral experience permitted him to obtain a clear picture of his Vaudois fellow-citizens who, though truly desiring to have the bishop thrown out, wished to limit themselves to what Viret called a *deformation* and refused all true *reformation* according to the Word of God:

> They gladly hear the preachers when they cry out against the sins of the priests and monks, but they don't want to hear them cry out against *their* sins. They want a Gospel preached without repentance and without a changed life. They want, under the name of the Gospel, a liberty which would be for them an unrestrained license to do anything they please. They truly desire to cast off the yoke of the Antichrist, but they want nothing to do with carrying Christ's.[15]

It was because he sought a Church practicing sanctification that Viret, in spite of his love for peace, was progressively drawn into a merciless wrestling match with the quasi-Roman power of the Bernese Republic. Roger Barilier, in his remarkable historical play *Viret Banished,* dedicated to the dramatic circumstances which we've examined, characterized Viret's thought so aptly by these words which he placed in the Reformer's mouth:

---

[15] Vuilleumier, *Notre Pierre Viret*, p. 143.

The Church will not be reformed; she shall not truly be the Church until the day when she will be emancipated from the civil power, when the authority of the ministry will be recognized, when she will be disciplined according to the Gospel, and when she will clearly confess, by her faith and by her works, the name of her glorious Savior.[16]

In Viret's satirical dialogue, *Le Monde à l'Empire et le Monde Démoniacle [The Corruption of the World's Empires and the World Demonized]*, we read:

> "The reformation of the Gospel can be understood in two ways."
>
> "How is this?"
>
> "We can truly take the reformation of the Gospel for a reformation by which men reform their lives and conversation to the rule of the Gospel. . . . But there is also another way, which could be called a *fake* or *illegitimate* reformation."
>
> "What do you mean by this fake or illegitimate reformation?"
>
> "A deliberate reformation in which men don't truly wish to reform their morals, their old and wicked customs, and their lifestyles to the rule of the Gospel, but they instead wish to reform the Gospel to *their* standard and to make it serve their desires and their personal gain and profit.[17]

Viret, no more than Calvin or Farel, Bullinger or Zwingli, desired a Church separated from the State. But, as Calvin himself (and even Farel) had done, after having welcomed as providential the support of the Bernese authorities in establishing the Reformation, the French-speaking Reformers quickly realized

---

[16] Roger Barilier, *Viret banni* (Cahiers de la Renaissance vaudoise, Lausanne, 1970), p. 177.

[17] Pierre Viret, *Le Monde à l'Empire et le Monde Démoniacle* (Geneva, 1561), p. 118. Quoted by Claude-Gilbert Dubois, *La conception de l'histoire en France au XVIe siecle (1560-1610)* (Nizet, Paris, 1977), p. 451.

the spiritual dangers which the political predominance of the State over the Church revealed. No true reformation of the Church and society can be achieved without the reestablishment of a true spiritual autonomy of the Church in relation to the State. This crucial independence is marked negatively by refusing the magistrate's interference in the internal life of the Church; positively by the reestablishment within the Church itself of a true ecclesiastical jurisdiction leading to the disciplinary power of the consistories, which must be expressed concretely in the right of excommunication of unbelievers and public sinners. Their Excellencies of Bern, in their slow but inflexible march toward absolute power, couldn't tolerate such pretensions for a single moment. This would signify the establishment of a state within the State, the manifestation of a power which—even in a small way—evaded their will of total ascendancy over society.

For Viret, the Church ought to respect the power of the magistrate as being directly instituted by God (just like the father of the family, which is a biblical model of all social organisms) and not reduce it to an inferior state, as had often been done by the papacy. Let's hear what he said:

> The Church possesses her own ministers and leaders, not to engage in things pertaining to the office of the civil magistrates but solely over those things which concern her ministry and her discipline. For the power which the Lord has given her (of which the power of the keys is a symbol) is confined within these limits. Thus, if she oversteps these bounds and if her ministers in any way usurp the office of the magistrates, they abuse their office and are not true ministers but are instead tyrants who usurp what in no way belongs to them.[18]

But, on the other hand:

> No ruler exists who possesses the right to issue laws

---
[18] Barnaud, *Pierre Viret*, p. 527.

concerning religion and the worship of God. . . . If a presumptuous ruler is found so bold as to desire to put an end to God's worship, none should obey him, under pain of obeying the devil.[19]

In 1551, several years before his departure from Lausanne, Viret could write these strong words on the limits of pastoral obedience:

> Such magistrates who dare to usurp spiritual power in this way . . . desire a liberty which will be for them nothing more than an unrestrained license. . . . They want to hold the poor ministers and preachers under their paw as their valets, to make them scurry about and act under their hand as they please. If the ministers do not wish to do this, . . . they immediately cry that such ministers are arrogant and are rebels who seek to usurp the position of the magistrate.[20]

Viret well knew that the medieval perspective, a perspective largely inherited by the Reformers, united the Church and civil society, thus submitting all citizens to the same ecclesiastical discipline. This common discipline, different from and more demanding than that exercised by the magistrate because it was concerned with and dealt with the heart of man, was not faithful to the Bible's teaching on the relations between the Church and the State and society in general. The vision of a homogeneous religiously-Christian society—that of Christendom, *Christianitas*—was a legacy of the ancient Latin *Romanitas* in which society, both temporal and spiritual, encompassed all citizens together. It drew its origins not from Scripture but instead from Aristotle's political vision of the *polis* as constituting a true social whole, both political and religious. This was the heritage of the viewpoint encompassing the ancient city, a model which included every citizen within itself, of which

---

[19] Barnaud, *Pierre Viret*, p. 528.
[20] Viret, *Le Monde à l'Empire*, pp. 267-268. Quoted in Barnaud, *Pierre Viret*, p. 479.

the Roman Empire was a striking example.

In this sense the *Christianitas* of the Middle Ages and the Reformation corresponded to a large extent with the *Romanitas* of the Empire. Here we find the teaching of Viret to be far in advance of that of his contemporaries, even those of the Reformed camp. And, more importantly, Viret was here more faithful to the model of the Church which we find in the Bible than the Christendom belonging to the Age of Faith, both Roman Catholic as well as Reformed. Viret sought to bring back a living, regenerated Church, disciplined by the Word, a truly Christian, confessional community. This Church, which would seek first faithfulness to the Kingdom of God, would then become the light of the world and the salt of the earth; its teachings—concretely put into practice by its members—would move on to affect all institutions of society (indirectly, certainly, but nevertheless powerfully), beginning with the State, in order that every social order, through the influence of the sanctification of faithful Christian citizens, might conform itself to the distinct and beautifully-ordained design of God for the entirety of His creatures.

Viret wrote:

> We will not set our gaze on the multitude but on moral virtue. For we greatly prefer to have a little flock of sheep who rule themselves according to the obedience of the Word of God than a truly great herd made up of dogs, swine, wolves, and foxes, mixed together with all sorts of beasts.[21]

Viret understood better than anyone the distinction necessary between the two swords, both deriving their authority from God, both submitted in their actions to the divine mandates of Scripture, but each within its own proper sphere exercising authority through the means suitable for it. To the question: "Why is it necessary for the Church to maintain its own discipline exercised by elders when a civil jurisdiction perfectly capable of

---

[21] Barnaud, *Pierre Viret*, p. 523.

exercising justice already exists?", Viret responded:

> Because the matters are of a different nature. That is why it is necessary that the functions belonging to the Church and to the administration of its polity are to be distinguished from those which belong to civil discipline and the republic. Otherwise there would be confusion if temporal things and spiritual things all were all placed together.[22]

Such a perspective rejected the entirely new Roman tyranny of *popes in short robes* (that of the Bernese), to whom the false reformation was nothing but a *deformation,* no less than it rejected the old Roman tyranny: that of the popes and their bishops in the *long robes* of clerical Rome. Both of these, each in its own way, were sources of modern totalitarian power, and it made little difference whether the sole absolute sovereign were royal or republican, imperial or papal, spiritual or temporal, Bernese or Roman.

> Instead of a pope in his long robe, they want to make another in a short robe, which must be feared much more than those whom they so condemn, if it once takes root and is received and upheld.[23]

And Viret, without difficulty, clearly drew the inevitable consequences of the appearance of such a power as that of Bern simultaneously possessing religious and secular authority. This is that ancient Roman power which, since the French Revolution, has reappeared on the world scene in all its ancient force under the form of the modern Hegelian State: sovereign, absolute, completely autonomous, not accountable to anyone,

---

[22] Robert Linder, *The Political Ideas of Pierre Viret* (Droz, Geneva, 1964), p. 122.
[23] Viret here joins, in a prophetic way, the so important battle waged by Rousas John Rushdoony against the totalitarian temptation to power which today more than ever characterizes the modern State. See Rousas John Rushdoony, *The Politics of Guilt and Pity* (Craig Press, Nutley, 1970); *Christianity and the State* (Ross House Books, Vallecito, 1986).

least of all God, and even less to His laws, both transcendent and immanent. This totalitarian State, without faith or law (as was so clearly foreseen by the supreme theoretician Friedrich Hegel, 1770-1831), has become a god walking on earth, a god which knows no boundaries to its power or justice to its law. Hear again the prophetic voice of Viret:

> If the full power of the Church is in the hands of the magistrates, they can cut it up and sew it back together as they please. They will have no need to take the sword they carry with them elsewhere. They will set up and take away ministers as it seems good to them. They will make them their servants. When they are drunk and angry, they sack them, as the fancy takes them. And in this way the wolves will line their coats with fleece within the Church, and the true pastors will be cast out. For tyrants will never allow anyone to tell them the truth.[24]

A contemporary theologian, Rousas John Rushdoony, who, like Viret, has consecrated his entire life to the practical application of the Law of God to all aspects of reality—both spiritual and temporal—in his study on the relationship between Christianity and the State before the Reformation, reached the same conclusions as our sixteenth-century Reformer:

> Unless the state is under the triune God, there is no hope for freedom for either the church or men. If the state is its own god and its own source of morality, then the state can do no wrong, and no man has then the right or freedom to differ from or to challenge the state.... The modern humanistic state is history's most jealous god, and it will tolerate no rivals.[25]

---

[24] Philippe Godet, *Pierre Viret* (Lausanne, 1892), p. 133.
[25] Rousas John Rushdoony, *Christianity and the State* (Ross House Books, Vallecito, CA, 1986), p. 187.

The confrontation with Bern was inevitable. Banished from his homeland, Viret returned to his work in Geneva. After two years of a greatly-appreciated ministry there, Viret's failing health obliged him to seek a milder climate in France in the spring of 1561. In this country he exercised his remarkable talents to the benefit of the churches of southern France, the city of Lyon and, finally (which was his last exile), in Bearn, the kingdom of Jeanne d'Albret (1528-1572), queen of Navarre.

Viret was a man of rare modesty. Posterity, in taking his misleading appreciation of himself at his word, greatly underestimated him. Here is an example of what some of his contemporaries said of his preaching gifts:

> His speech was so sweet that he continually held the attention and the interest of those who heard him. His style, which united strength to harmony, was so caressing to the ear and to the mind that even those of his hearers least interested in religious matters, those most impatient of other preachers, would hear him out without difficulty and even with pleasure. It was said that his listeners were as it were suspended on his lips, wishing his discourses were even longer.[26]

Melchior Adam gave his opinion:

> In Lyon, preaching out in the open, he brought thousands to saving faith in Jesus Christ. By the power of his divine eloquence he even caused those passing by to stop, listen, and remain until he had finished.[27]

Of Calvin Beza wrote, "None have taught with greater authority;" of Farel, "None thundered more mightily than he;" but of Viret he confessed, "None has a more winsome charm

---

[26] Barnaud, *Pierre Viret*, pp. 539-540.
[27] Barnaud, *Pierre Viret*, p. 540.

when he speaks."[28] Some of his contemporaries placed him above Calvin as a preacher.

But if Calvin is incomparable as a dogmatic exegete and polemicist, Viret greatly surpasses him as ethicist and apologist.[29] His strength was a domain often neglected because of its difficulty: the application of the Word of God to all domains of life, that spirit of prophecy which the Revelation unites to the preaching of the Gospel: "the testimony of Jesus is the spirit of prophecy" (Rev. 19:10). This "spirit of prophecy" is the application of the red-hot iron of the Law-Word of God to the sins of the world.

Viret's *Christian Instruction in the Doctrine of the Law and Gospel* of 1564 unquestionably contains the best commentary on the Ten Commandments that the Christian Church has ever known.[30] Within the third and fourth volumes of this *Christian Instruction,* Pierre Viret, as if he had the premonition of the apparition of the philosophical idealism of Descartes (a subjectivism that doesn't allow any true link between the knowledge of nature and that of the Creator, Romans 1:18-23), gives us a magisterial application of the Biblical doctrine of the general revelation of God throughout all creation. His marvelous polemical dialogue, *Le Monde à l'Empire et le Monde Démoniacle* (1561) contains—among many other treasures—a historical, social, and economic analysis of his time through the light of the Word of

---

[28] Vuilleumier, *Notre Pierre Viret,* p. 142.

[29] Very few of Viret's works are available in modern editions. For a listing of the available English translations of his works, see the list facing the title page of this book. For editions of his works in French, see *Pierre Viret d'après lui-meme* (Bridel, Lausanne, 1911); Pierre Viret, *Quatre sermons français sur Esaie 65* (Payot, Lausanne, 1961); Pierre Viret, *Deux Dialogues: L'Alcumie de Purgatoire. L'Homme naturel* (Bibliotèque romande, Lausanne, 1971). The labors of the Association Pierre Viret have begun to fill this gap. It has, among others, published the three first volumes of Viret's *Instruction chrétienne* (L'Age d'Homme, Lausanne). Roxandra Vulcan has edited one of Viret's earliest works, *Dialogues du désordre qui est à présent au monde* (Labor et Fides, Geneva, 2012).

[30] This work has been translated into English and published in ten volumes by Psalm 78 Ministries under the titles: Pierre Viret, *No Other God; Nothing Like God; Taking His Name in Vain; Remember the Sabbath Day; Honor Thy Father and Mother; Thou Shalt Not Kill; Thou Shalt Not Commit Adultery; Thou Shalt Not Steal; Defend the Truth;* and *Thou Shalt Not Covet.*

God. This permits him, for example, to put his finger on the operation of certain perverted economic phenomena two centuries before the development of modern economic science! As a Christian moralist he was comparable to a John Chrysostom of the fifth century, to a Lancelot Andrewes at the beginning of the seventeenth century, to a Benedict Pictet in the eighteenth, to a Cardinal Pie at the end of the nineteenth, and also to a Rousas John Rushdoony of our own day. It is high time that we finally begin to grasp the importance of what a remarkable thinker Pierre Viret was, and that we vigorously pursue the republication of his works in modern editions. We must return to his vision of the application of the entire Word of God to all aspects of human life and to all scientific disciplines in order that we might bring all prideful thoughts of man's rebellion against God captive to the obedience of Christ and His Law (2 Cor. 10:4-5). Without such a return to such Biblical realism, we can have no hope for the revival of the Church and for the restoration of its reformational influence over the entirety of culture and society.

To conclude this too brief survey, I will give you the words of a man who knew Pierre Viret well and who, moving beyond the modesty of his friend, placed him among the greatest men of God, those humble and powerful servants by which the Lord Jesus Christ is glorified in His Church. This is what Theodore Beza wrote of Pierre Viret in his *Portraits* of 1581:

Pierre Viret

I see his body, beaten, fraught with suffering and age,
Recipient of poison, wounds, and all man's deadly rage.
I see the power of the Lord, His noble mysteries,
And in great silence I submit myself to His decrees.

I read the precious writings, full of wisdom without end,
That you, my dearest Viret, in that dreadful prison penned.
I see the goodness of your judgment and your conscience clear,
And know that truly God resides within your mansion here.

I know Christ watches o'er His Church with gentle, loving care,
For, seeing it half-dead, engulfed in flame, in great despair,
He lights a fire within men's souls within that dreadful heat,
Enflaming hearts, enlight'ning minds, to make His Church complete.

If all the folly of the world rejects His sacred way,
Demanding from us some new sign, some miracle today,
Our gentle Viret will provide a witness with each breath;
He spoke to them in life, and he is speaking still in death.[31]

---

[31] Theodore de Beze, *Les vrais portraits des hommes illustres* (translated from the Latin to French by Simon Goulart, Slatkine, Geneva, 1986 [1581]), p. 128.

CHAPTER TWO

Pierre Viret and the Knowledge of God

In expounding the subject of *Pierre Viret the theologian*, I have asked myself how to begin such a vast and diverse topic. To properly treat a theme of such magnitude, a certain number of fields must first be mastered:

(1) We must know, understand, and jointly consider all the written work of the Vaudois Reformer. Who could be capable of grasping the contents of a work which includes many tens of thousands of pages?

(2) But, even more, in order to truly understand Viret's theology, we must be able to determine what the sources of his theology are and their respective roles in the constitution of his work.

(3) Further, in order to assess its true scope, we must place his theology within the setting of his predecessors: first the patristic and scholastic writers; then the generation which preceded him: Erasmus of Rotterdam, Martin Luther, and the spiritual movement and educational system of the Brethren of the Common Life which so strongly marked that entire generation; William Farel at Neuchatel, Martin Bucer at Strasbourg, then the Reformed theologians of German Switzerland at Bern, Basel, and eastern Switzerland; and finally his contemporaries and immediate successors: Heinrich Bullinger at Zurich, John Calvin at Geneva, and the men marked by his influence: his longtime colleague, Theodore Beza, Zacharius Ursinus, Olevianus, and Guido de Bres, who were his students for a time.

(4) Finally, we must master the part of the immense

secular culture to which the entire work of this great Vaudois Reformer testifies.

It's clear that I am quite incapable—and that I always will be—of comprehending and encompassing, from these different perspectives, such a rich, vast, and complex work!

Thus, how can I attempt to expound the theme which has been assigned to me: *Pierre Viret the Theologian?* Fortunately two authors, Anne-Marie Salgat and Georges Bavaud, have already carefully examined various aspects of Pierre Viret's theology and can truly come to our aid.

A) In 1972 Anne-Marie Salgat defended a doctoral thesis on the subject: *Aspects of the Life and Theology of Pierre Viret (1511-1571).*[1] We will greatly draw from the second part of this work, pages 81-321, the section of her thesis in which she describes Pierre Viret's theology.

B) The canon Georges Bavaud, a great Vaudois specialist of Viret's work, published an essential work in 1986 entitled: *Le Réformateur Pierre Viret (1511-1571): Sa Théologie.*[2] We find here the fruit of years of attentive reading of the works of the Vaudois Reformer from the perspective of a Roman Catholic strongly attached to both the modern and ancient traditions of his Church.

Thus, though the following exposition that I will give of Pierre Viret's theology is marked by a long—though certainly incomplete—acquaintance with his work, yet I will also strongly lean upon these two solid studies.

And what about the subject itself, so vast and so complex, both beautifully ordered and also marked by a spirit of such great balance, of such delicacy, and such exemplary stability? How then should I begin? When I think about it, it seems to me that the simplest way appears to be to take the definition which the ancients gave of theology: *theos* and *logos,* the word concerning God, or the *knowledge,* the *science* of God. It's in

---

[1] Union Theological Seminary, New York, 1972.
[2] Labor et Fides, Geneva, 1986.

this sense that the Greek fathers considered the Apostle John as *the Theologian* above all, the evangelist who delivered to us the revealed knowledge of God *par excellence*. It's in this same sense that the ancients took Gregory of Nazianzus, who expressed with such sublimity the Trinity and the incarnation of the Son of God, as the *Theologian par excellence*. This is also the way that the Greek tradition considered the great Byzantine doctor of the Church of the tenth and eleventh centuries, Simeon (949-1022), the successor of St. Gregory, ascribing to him the title of the *New Theologian*. A dictionary of the Christian Church expressed this subject in this way:

> His appellation "the New" or "Younger Theologian" ranks him as second in Byzantine estimation to St. Gregory Nazianzus, "The Theologian" *par excellence.*[3]

Thus for this chapter we will now limit ourselves to one subject, already far too vast for the space provided to us: *what Pierre Viret taught on the knowledge of God.*

WHAT PIERRE VIRET TAUGHT ON THE KNOWLEDGE OF GOD

How can we know God?

This question of the possibility of a true knowledge of God, even if it is limited by and accommodated to our finiteness, our nature as a creature, and by the effects of sin on our mind and understanding, isn't a question that Pierre Viret even begins to consider.[4] There are for him two clear ways leading to a true knowledge of God: Holy Scripture and creation, the Bible and the established order of nature. Thus he dismisses two false foundations: a Church which claims infallibility and its counterpart, Tradition, a source of salvific truth equal to the

---

[3] F. L. Cross, ed., *The Oxford Dictionary of the Christian Church* (Oxford University Press, London, 1966 [1957]), p. 1256.

[4] Viret stands here—like the other theologians of the Reformation—in a pre-critical, pre-Cartesian and pre-Kantian tradition, that is, prior to the development and cultural domination of the mathematical and experimental sciences.

Bible. Neither Church nor Tradition, according to him, possesses a direct mediatorial function between God and men. Let's hear how Georges Bavaud summarizes his thought on this:

> ... the Reformer speaks of "two books which God has given us to teach us and to lead us to the knowledge of Him," which are "the book of nature" and "the book of His Word."[5]

Yet Viret certainly favored God's special revelation through His Word over His revelation in His creation:

> Even though He has revealed His great power, wisdom, and goodness to us through all visible things, ... yet He reveals it much more clearly and intimately to us through His Word and His Holy Scriptures.[6]

Thus, founded on God's general revelation in His creation and, even more, on His special revelation—the Bible—Viret affirms that man, even sinful man, can know God. But if for him the divine essence infinitely surpasses the limited nature of the creature, yet it can nevertheless be known by man. This is his description of the knowledge of the divinity that man has received. What is God for Viret? Let's hear what he says:

> I mean a spiritual and divine essence, eternal, free and at full liberty, true, good, just, pure, unpolluted, holy, possessing understanding, perfect in mercy and every virtue, and who is of infinite power, wisdom, and goodness, more than could ever be expressed, imagined, or comprehended in any way at all, even by all the creatures together.[7]

Thus Pierre Viret affirms the complete *transcendence*

---

[5] Bavaud, *Le Réformateur Pierre Viret*, p. 18.
[6] Pierre Viret, *Instruction chrétienne*, Vol. II, p. 380, quoted in Bavaud, *Le Réformateur Pierre Viret*, p. 18.
[7] Bavaud, *Le Réformateur Pierre Viret*, p. 49.

of God—God infinitely surpasses all His creatures—and His *immanence,* His presence within every aspect of His creation. He is above all and present everywhere. We here find ourselves presented with one of the most indispensable tools for the practice of theology: the affirmation of two Biblical truths which might appear contradictory from the viewpoint of a binary, univocal, and far too simplistic logic—the *either/or*—but which are, in fact, complementary. Truly God is utterly transcendent, separate from His creation, but at the same time He is universally immanent, present everywhere in His creation. In other words, in His personal essence *(ad intra)* He is unknowable ("No man hath seen God at any time"), and by His external acts *(ad extra),* by the revelation of His uncreated grace (the Orthodox would say "by His *energies*"), He makes Himself known to man by His works (creation and providence) and by His Word, His Son made man. "And this is life eternal, that they might know thee the only true God, and Jesus Christ, whom thou hast sent" (John 17:3).

Let's go one step further. For Viret a direct knowledge (the philosophical term is *univocal)* of the divine essence is impossible for man. Yet, according to Pierre Viret, God makes Himself known by revealing Himself to men; thus he here equally rejects theological skepticism (the philosophical position known as *equivocity)* and the claim to a direct "univocal" view of God. Thus this is a double rejection: that of skepticism about God on the one hand and that of every direct "clear and distinct (Descartes)" vision of God on the other. He rejects the attitude according to which the human mind is incapable of knowing anything certain about God; but he also rejects that of an immediate, clear, and independent intellectual hold on God.

How then can we truly know God? In order to know Him we must go beyond the *univocal* and *equivocal* ways. One option still remains to be recovered—under different terms— from the fathers of the first centuries, from the scholastic doctors of the Middle Ages, from the Reformers of the sixteenth and seventeenth centuries, and also from the Orthodox tradition: we cannot access God through our own efforts as finite and sinful creatures. It is God who, by grace, reveals Himself to us in His merciful goodness. He comes to us, not in His essence, by nature unknowable to the creature, but by His "divine energies," graces which work *ad extra*—we could say—outside the essence of the divinity; the Orthodox say "by condescending" to us; by an "analogy," preserving the distance between the Creator and the creature, as scholasticism notes; and in a manner "accommodated" to our weakness (the Reformed position). Bavaud very clearly expresses the position which Pierre Viret defends:

> Viret never employed the term "analogy," but in fact he turned to this way in order to avoid, faced with God, the two opposing errors of agnosticism [equivocity: God cannot be known] and anthropomorphism [univocity: we can know God in the same way that we know His creatures, in a "clear and distinct" direct manner].[8]

But, in order for God to speak to men, He must employ their language, a language which is analogical: true but adapted, accommodated to human capacities. This is how Viret speaks to us of the necessity of God using our own human and earthly language:

> Because, for lack of more suitable terms, we are forced to use and borrow these words from the common speech of mankind in order that by a similarity with human and understandable things we might more easily express heavenly and divine things which surpass and exceed our slow-witted and ignorant minds, which can't understand any loftier language. By doing this we follow the example that the Spirit of God sets forth for us in the Holy Scriptures, in which He not only speaks to us but, when speaking to us by them, He condescends to the smallness, feebleness, weakness, and limited capacity of our minds by using human language accommodated to our understanding

---

[8] Bavaud, *Le Réformateur Pierre Viret*, p. 50.

when speaking of divine things, as if He spoke of human and natural things. Therefore we must truly beware of abusing and misusing this great blessing and condescension which this good God uses with us just as a gentle, kind, and loving father who stammers with his young children in order to accommodate himself to their tender age.[9]

What difference of tone we see in this quite Viretian way of considering accommodation as opposed to that which his excellent co-laborer and friend, John Calvin, occasionally uses. Let's look at a page of Calvin's *Commentary on the Book of Genesis* in which the Genevan Reformer describes the creation of the two great lights, the sun and the moon:

> I have said, that Moses does not here subtilely descant, as a philosopher, on the secrets of nature, as may be seen in these words. First, he assigns a place in the expanse of heaven to the planets and stars; but astronomers make a distinction of spheres, and, at the same time, teach that the fixed stars have their proper place in the firmament. Moses makes two great luminaries; but astronomers prove, by conclusive reasons, that the star of Saturn, which, on account of its great distance, appears the least of all, is greater than the moon. Here lies the difference; *Moses wrote in a popular style things which, without instruction, all ordinary persons, endued with common sense, are able to understand;* but astronomers investigate with great labour whatever the sagacity of the human mind can comprehend. Nevertheless, this study is not to be reprobated, nor this science to be condemned, because some frantic persons are wont boldly to reject whatever is unknown to them. For astronomy is not only pleasant, but also very useful to be known: it cannot be denied that this art unfolds this admirable wisdom of God. Wherefore, *as ingenious men are to*

---
[9] Pierre Viret, *Marvelous Trinity: the Believer's Hope and Delight* (Psalm 78 Ministries, Monticello, FL, 2019), pp. 39-40.

> *be honoured who have expended useful labour on this subject,* so they who have leisure and capacity ought not to neglect this kind of exercise. Nor did Moses truly wish to withdraw us from this pursuit in omitting such things as are peculiar to the art; but because he was ordained a teacher as well of the unlearned and rude as of the learned, he could not otherwise fulfill his office than by *descending to this grosser method of instruction.* Had he spoken of things generally unknown, *the uneducated* might have pleaded in excuse that such subjects were beyond their capacity.[10]

Charles Simeon (1759-1836), the great Anglican theologian and preacher of Reformed confessional convictions, truly put his finger on this difference of expression between Calvin and the Biblical authors as well as between Calvin and Viret. He distinguishes here between a more intellectual aspect and the simplicity of the Scriptures. Charles Simeon, in a series of sermons preached at Cambridge University—the highest intellectual authority in the kingdom—spoke these words on the value of the Anglican liturgy:

> Let me then speak the truth before God: Though I am no Arminian, I do think that the refinements of Calvin have done great harm in the church: they have driven multitudes from the plain and popular way of speaking used by the inspired writers, and have made them unreasonably and unscripturally squeamish in their modes of expression; and I conceive that, the less addicted any person is to systematic accuracy, the more he will accord with the inspired writers, and the more he will approve of the views of our Reformers.[11]

---

[10] John Calvin, *Commentaries on the First Book of Moses Called Genesis* (John King, trans., Baker Books, Grand Rapids, MI, 2005), pp. 86-87. Emphasis added.

[11] Charles Simeon, "The Excellency of the Liturgy," in *Horae homileticae, or Discourses now first digested into one Continued Series and forming a commentary upon every book of the Old and New Testament, Volume II: Numbers to Joshua* (Henry Bohn, London, 1846), p. 259.

For Viret, therefore, man can know God through His works of creation and redemption. The language of the Bible which speaks to us of these divine works is an adequate means to communicate such a knowledge to men. Let's hear our Vaudois Reformer one more time:

> And, because we can't ever understand this essence and its nature except as much as He has revealed it to us by the revelation of His will and His works, the main thing that we are required to believe and which we must most diligently inquire into are these two last points which, with the first, are set forth in this [Apostles] creed....
>
> We'll consider this work particularly in two things which include all the others—that is, the work of creation and then of redemption.[12]

Let's take a moment to follow the steps of Pierre Viret in this conversation where, through an animated discussion between the disciple (Nathaniel) and his teacher (Philip), he explains the contents of the Apostles Creed. After having laid down the distinction between living faith (which personally possesses the contents of the faith) and dead faith (which possesses no more than an intellectual knowledge of this faith without applying it to one's life), Viret continues:

> NATHANIEL: I'm quite satisfied concerning this point. Now tell me who this God is in whom you believe. For I've decided to ask you about each point individually, not like a member of the Inquisition to examine your faith and conscience, but that I might learn and might be instructed by you.
>
> PHILIP: You ask me something that no mind could ever comprehend, nor could any tongue explain it according to its dignity and worth.

---

[12] Viret, *Marvelous Trinity*, p. 35.

NATHANIEL: Why then do you call Him God if no tongue can utter His name?

PHILIP: It's quite true that many names are ascribed to Him among all peoples, languages, and nations, but there are none that can perfectly define, comprehend, and express His nature, essence, divinity, virtue, and majesty.

NATHANIEL: Then what are these names good for?

PHILIP: They assist the weakness and ignorance of men, who must speak of God according to what their meager understanding is able to comprehend and understand sufficiently for their salvation. On this you must note that, in order to understand what is necessary for us to understand, we must in the first place consider three things in order to obtain such an understanding as we must have and know about our God.

NATHANIEL: What are these things?

PHILIP: The first is His essence. The second is His will. The third is His work.
    Concerning His essence, we must consider His unity; and then, in this unity, the trinity of persons of the Father and the Son and the Holy Spirit in the same essence and divinity. And, . . . we can't ever understand this essence and its nature except as much as He has revealed it to us by the revelation of His will and His works, . . .[13]

The conversation continues:

PHILIP: Now what I say of His will is nearly the same as what I understand by His work, for the work reveals the will.

---

[13] Viret, *Marvelous Trinity*, pp. 34-35.

He goes on:

> PHILIP: We'll consider this work particularly in two things which include all the others—that is, the work of creation and then of redemption. Whoever truly understands these things as they are set forth in this creed understands what is necessary to know of God both for his own salvation as well as for honoring Him as He must be honored.[14]

And Viret, through this most captivating conversation between Philip the teacher and Nathaniel the disciple, deals with the following points:

— The divine essence and the nature of God; and the trinity of persons within it

— The fatherhood of God the Father toward Jesus Christ His Son, and toward the creatures, and particularly toward man

— The rules which it is suitable to follow in the consideration of the essence and nature of God and of His works; and how Jesus Christ is the Son of God

— The loftiness and profundity of the mysteries of the trinity of divine persons in the essence of God; and the language of the Holy Spirit in this matter; and the reason for it

— The similarity and difference which exists between the divine generation of the Son of God and the human conception of men

— How no appropriate language or suitable example exists to clearly express the trinity of divine persons within the essence of God and the divine generation within it; and how examples taken from creatures—particularly the sun—can assist us in this

— The appropriate way to consider the properties of the divine persons in the essence of God; and in what sense the Son is called the Word

— The similarity which exists between the conception

---
[14] Viret, *Marvelous Trinity*, p. 35.

and the nature and effects of a human word and the divine and eternal Word, which is the true Son of God

— The dissimilarity and difference which must be considered in the preceding similarity and comparison between the divine and human word

— How this same example and comparison can also assist in the distinction of the divine person of the Holy Spirit

— How David's words agree with those of Moses concerning the work of the persons of the Trinity in the creation of the world; and why he didn't list either more or fewer divine persons in the essence of God

— The fatherhood of God toward His creatures and particularly toward mankind

— How the name "Father" ascribed to God means more than the name "Creator"; and how God is the Father of the elect

— The providence of God

— The power and will of God

— Believers' assurance in the power and will of God

— The necessity between the first cause, which is God, and second causes, which are the natural order that He has established among the creatures

— The difference between the doctrine and knowledge of faith and human reason and philosophy in the matter of God's providence; and the testimonies of God in His miraculous works by which He testifies that His power and freedom aren't subject to or bound by second causes

— Other testimonies from the Holy Scripture dealing with the same subject

— The invocation of angels and saints; and trust placed in them

You can truly see that Viret's teaching takes on impressive proportions even on this single question of the knowledge of God alone. It isn't possible for me to deal in an adequate manner with all this material here. I'll simply draw your attention to one or two points. We see first the two rules that Viret sets down in order to correctly consider God.

> PHILIP: To better understand this whole subject, we must truly note two rules which are suitable for us to follow and practice.
>
> NATHANIEL: What are they?
>
> PHILIP: The first is that every time and whenever we consider the divinity in itself, we must distinguish between the persons of the Trinity which exist within it. But, when we contrast it with the creatures and make a comparison of it with them, then we only speak of one eternal essence.
>
> NATHANIEL: What is the second?
>
> PHILIP: When it's a question of the works of God, and particularly the creation and redemption of mankind and other similar things which are outside of this divinity, we must consider and receive them as works done in common by all the persons within this divine essence. For the Father and the Son and the Holy Spirit don't work on their own, separated from each other, but they all labor together—the Father by the Son and the Holy Spirit, by whom the Father and the Son reveal their power.[15]

Then he poses a capital question:

> NATHANIEL: How [is] Jesus Christ Son of God?
>
> PHILIP: You must know that Jesus Christ is Son of God with regard to His divinity because He is eternally begotten of the Father and is of the same essence and substance with Him. And, concerning His humanity, He is also truly His Son because He was conceived in the womb of the virgin by the working of the Holy

---
[15] Viret, *Marvelous Trinity*, pp. 37-38.

Spirit, without any human seed, by a miraculous conception and generation different than all other men.[16]

We can see the great wisdom that Pierre Viret reveals in these two principles which he establishes from Scripture:

(1) On the one hand, when we consider God in Himself, we must truly be careful to distinguish the divine persons from each other. When we contrast God with His creatures, however, we must then place the emphasis on the unity of the divinity and the difference between the divine essence and His creatures, between God and His creation.

(2) On the other hand, when we more specifically consider God's working outside of Himself, we must then pay attention to the fact that the three Persons of the Trinity are always active together, each working in the way which is proper to Him.

By respecting these two rules (in themselves quite simple), we will avoid many errors in interpreting biblical texts.

Let's take another example from the theological wisdom of Viret's thought on God. Here is what is said in this *Simple Exposition of the Apostles Creed* on "The Power and the Will of God." Concerning the creed's affirmation of the almighty power of God, Nathaniel asks:

NATHANIEL: Why do we say *Almighty*?

PHILIP: We say this to show that this Father is truly different than our earthly fathers who can't do anything of themselves; but He can do all He pleases, both in heaven and on earth.

Then Viret brings along a full series of biblical quotations to reinforce this doctrine of God's omnipotence. Nathaniel then asks:

NATHANIEL: And how does the knowledge that He

---
[16] Viret, *Marvelous Trinity*, p. 38.

is almighty benefit us?

> PHILIP: This knowledge gives us a strong assurance and brings a wondrous peace to our hearts and consciences. For, if we're assured that He is our Father (particularly because He has adopted us by His Son Jesus Christ), we can't doubt His good will and His paternal affection for us. Thus, because we are already assured of His good will, we must never fear that He will fail to put this will into effect since He possesses the power to do so.[17]

You see how, according to Pierre Viret the theologian, even the loftiest doctrine of God (here His almighty power) is immediately brought into service for the benefit of believers. The theologian is most certainly also always a pastor, a shepherd of the flock. Let's hear the remainder of this beautiful conversation.

> NATHANIEL: It's very difficult for a man to be able to do anything if he doesn't possess these two things together: the will and the power. For what good is a will without ability or power? And what good does power serve if no will exists?

> PHILIP: Therefore, when we call Him Father, we simultaneously confess that we are assured of the goodwill and affection that He has for us. And, in order that we might understand that His will isn't vain and doesn't exist without being put into effect, we ascribe to Him all power. These things teach us that He isn't like a mortal man who often wills something but is unable to do it, and that He doesn't resemble a tyrant or some rich and powerful man who could do many things if he wanted to but his will isn't in agreement with his power.

> NATHANIEL: Thus, from what you say, it follows that God doesn't retain His power within Himself

---

[17] Viret, *Marvelous Trinity*, p. 60.

> like a miser or like a moneylender hoards his riches and his treasures without ever distributing them to anyone, but instead that He continually puts it to use among His creatures.
>
> PHILIP: This is exactly what I'm trying to say. For, when we acknowledge and confess Him to be almighty (according to the testimony that He gives us of His power in His Word), we don't speak of this power only according to what exists in His essence and divinity alone, but more specifically according to how He reveals it and puts it to work among His creatures. For this is the way by which He reveals and displays what would otherwise be concealed from us in Himself. Thus, when we confess that He is almighty, we confess that all creatures are subject to Him and that He disposes of them and leads and governs them as He pleases, in such a way that nothing can hinder Him.[18]

Finally, let's consider the way in which Pierre Viret deals with the question so debated during the final centuries of the Middle Ages concerning the relation between omnipotent divine power and the laws of this created order established by Him—that is, the relation between the First Cause and second causes. To put it another way, how can the extraordinary miracles of God be reconciled with the natural course of the laws of the created order? Listen to Nathaniel, the student, pose the problem:

> NATHANIEL: When I consider all these things with greater diligence, I find many more errors and vast deceptions in the minds of men which would be easy to uproot if we possessed in our hearts more of this faith that we confess with our mouth instead of this hypocrisy that you just mentioned. And, in order that I might hear your opinion on this, I'll mention a few of those which come to my mind at present.
>   We've spoken of those who deny the provi-

---

[18] Viret, *Marvelous Trinity*, p. 61.

dence and forethought of God, but it seems to me that there is also another type of people opposed to these who are yet in an error scarcely less than them.

Who then are these thinkers who distort the designs of God in this way?

> NATHANIEL: For, instead of (like the first [the Epicureans]) thinking that God leaves all to happen at random without caring for or concerning Himself about anything at all, these others [the Stoics] think to the contrary that God placed a certain natural order among His creatures which can never be changed; but that all things must necessarily happen according to this order which He once for all ordained from the beginning [these immutable laws of the creational or natural order, absolutely necessary, thus excluding any possibility of a miracle].

He continues:

> NATHANIEL: In this I think in one way they have a much better opinion than the agnostics have [or the Epicureans, whose false god doesn't worry himself about anything], which is the fact that they acknowledge some providence of God. But it seems to me that they greatly err in the fact that they force and bind God (who is the first cause of everything) to second causes [the laws claimed to be strictly necessary and absolute for nature] and to His creatures and to the first ordinance that He gave them in this way, and that they deprive Him of all power or ability to change anything at all and to dispose of things other than He did at the beginning.[19]

And what is the moral and spiritual consequence of such a belief?

---

[19] Viret, *Marvelous Trinity*, pp. 63-64.

> NATHANIEL: For this reason, when they find themselves in some danger which is so great that it's impossible for the human mind to find a solution or a way among men or among any of the other creatures to be able to escape from it, they are immediately so tormented by the thought and the belief they have in natural causes that they fall into despair and think that there is no hope of escape from the evils that have come upon them, for they think that nature works all things and that it always follows its path according to the order that God once for all established, without Him ever involving Himself in it anymore.

Faced with the omnipresent cultural domination of the modern scientific view of a world ordained by necessity by the immutable laws of science, this manner of posing the problem of the freedom God possesses to work even within the course of this nature whose stable order, established by Him, is constantly upheld by His almighty power, is a truly and surprisingly relevant topic. The teacher responds:

> PHILIP: This error proceeds from the school of the stoics and other similar philosophers who are truly of the opinion that God assists the creatures. But they have so bound Him to this natural order (which they call *second causes* which are dependent on Him, who is the *first cause*), that they've deprived Him of all power and freedom. For they (great philosophers that they were!) didn't understand that no matter what order or arrangement God has placed in nature, yet He is never bound or subject to it or to any creature whatever. To the contrary, He always works in full freedom and supports and upholds His creatures by His power and by His goodness and mercy (Acts 17:26).

Thus God isn't in any way imprisoned within the laws of the established order created and sustained by Him from the beginning:

PHILIP: Therefore, even though He follows the order that He placed in nature, yet if He wills to punish or chastise men for their sins or rescue them and do them good in order to reveal His goodness to them, He easily changes this order when He chooses to, and alters it and makes it serve His will just as much as He pleases, as we have examples of in all the miracles that Holy Scripture mentions (Acts 17:26).

NATHANIEL: I think that these people have fallen into this error because they are afraid of making God mutable, who is by nature immutable; otherwise He wouldn't be God (Mal. 3:6).

PHILIP: I believe it's true. But it doesn't follow from this that God is mutable. For, if there is any change, it isn't in Him and doesn't come from within Him or from His will, which is immutable, but from us who are mutable and from the fact that we can't understand or comprehend the decisions and conclusions of His eternal and immutable counsel or the means He uses to put them into execution. Therefore, no matter what He has ordained, we mustn't cease to call on Him to always fulfill our duty to Him according to the vocation to which He has called us and the means that He has given us.

NATHANIEL: I agree with you. And it seems to me that all those [Stoics] who hold such an opinion of God don't believe that He is the Creator and almighty Father, for they limit His power.[20]

Viret then examines the difference which exists on the one hand between "the doctrine and the knowledge of faith" and, on the other hand, "reason and human philosophy" on the subject of "God's providence." Let's again listen to this very illuminating conversation:

---

[20] Viret, *Marvelous Trinity*, pp. 64-65.

> PHILIP: By this you can understand the difference which exists between the knowledge that a person acquires by his human reason and that which is given to him by faith, which sees and understands what human reason can't see or understand. Therefore we must always take the Word of God as our guide in these things and judge according to it and not according to our own fancies or according to the opinions and dreams of the philosophers.

He explains:

> For, though the work of creation . . . ought to be more than sufficient to confirm us in this belief, yet because the human mind blinded by sin can't see as clearly as it could see if it hadn't fallen into such darkness as it's fallen into, God, having pity and compassion on mankind, truly desired to set before his eyes other works than those which He had already accomplished in the creation and ordering of all things, and by another means and in another way than those which He ordained in nature from the beginning. By this He has, as it were, created another new world, revealing that He hasn't lost His power or subjected His freedom to His creatures [i.e., to the laws of nature] but instead that He is always able to work either by them or apart from them, according to His own pleasure.

Then, through his spokesman Philip, Viret supplies examples of this miraculous work of God:

> PHILIP: We have examples of this particularly in the miraculous works that were done in Egypt by the hands of Moses; and then at the Red Sea and the passage through it; and in the desert in the manna sent from heaven; and in the water taken out of the rock; and other similar events (Ex. 7:1-11:10; 12:29; 13:21-22; 14:16-22; 15:6-11; 16:4, 10-13; Jer. 6:19; 1 Cor. 10:1-4; 2 Cor. 3:17). You can be quite certain

that these works weren't accomplished according to the common and general order and course of nature but by a new and extraordinary way which neither the stoics nor all those who follow their beliefs could ever have thought of or hoped for.

He continues:

> We can judge the same of all the other miraculous and supernatural works that God worked both through the hands and the ministry of His prophets as well as through Jesus Christ His Son and His apostles and through all His other servants and ministers. . . . For these [miraculous acts] aren't natural means. Nor did they proceed from natural and second causes.[21]

But this supernatural and miraculous creation of God doesn't only affect the sphere of physical, material second causes. God also works in this extraordinary way in the psychological human sphere and within history:

> PHILIP: It's also written that the Lord removes the spirit and understanding of rulers and their counselors, and that He holds the king's heart in His hand just like the rivers and courses of water, and that He turns it wherever it pleases Him. . . . By these words He shows that He can turn their heart and their desires and alter them as He wills, regardless of their natural disposition.

After having given various examples in which we see the supernatural divine assistance granted to believers, Viret continues:

> PHILIP: All these passages testify that God provides for His own by other means than ordinary ones,

---

[21] Pierre Viret, *Exposition familière sur le symbole des apotres* (Jacques Berthet, Geneva, 1560), pp. 82-86.

assisting them even when all ordinary, natural, and human means fail them.

Then Viret ends, according to his theological habit, in a truly pastoral way:

> PHILIP: Therefore Jesus Christ said that we will obtain all that we request in faith: "If ye shall say unto this mountain, Be thou removed, and be thou cast into the sea; it shall be done" (Matt. 21:21). And in John: "He that believeth on Me, the works that I do shall he do also; and greater works than these shall he do; because I go unto My Father. And whatsoever ye shall ask in My name, that will I do" (John 14:12-13). Paul also said on this subject that God can give aid and "is able to do exceeding abundantly above all that we ask or think," for "of Him, and through Him, and to Him, are all things" (Eph. 3:20; Rom. 11:36).
>
> All these verses show us that God can aid and assist us even though second and natural causes and all human means not only fail us but also threaten us with ruin and utmost perdition.[22]

We won't follow Viret in his examination of the attributes of God—immutability, sensibility, love, jealousy, wrath, eternity, and many others. Viret defends the impassibility, immutability, aseity (God has no need of anything or anyone), simplicity (He possesses nothing within Himself which can be separated) of God and many other traditional attributes of the divinity. On the immutability of God, Viret writes:

> All the motions that He has are without any change either of time, place, or in any other way, in such a way that He always remains immutable.[23]

But, if God is truly impassible, if—as the Bible so strongly

---

[22] Viret, *Marvelous Trinity*, pp. 66-67.
[23] Pierre Viret, *Instruction chrétienne*, Vol. II, p. 857.

affirms—there is within Him "no variableness, neither shadow of turning" (Jam. 1:17), yet, as the Scripture also says, the triune God without doubt possesses sentiments: love, mercy, compassion, jealously, hatred, wrath, fury. Here is what Viret writes on this subject:

> Even though He is impassible in such a way that He can never tolerate evil or be inflamed with any passion like us, yet, with regards to us, He possesses these affections suitable to His nature and to ours. Thus all human emotions are ascribed to Him in the Holy Scriptures for the same reasons that we've already said that the members of a human body are also ascribed to Him. And, because we can't truly understand these divine emotions within the divine nature, He has set forth a living image for us in the human nature of His Son Jesus Christ.[24]

It is not without true analogy of proportion[25] that the perfect humanity of the Son of God incarnate is affirmed by Scripture to be the very image of the invisible God. Therefore many human qualities can serve as adequate expressions (without in any way being univocal!) to speak of God with an appropriate accuracy (accommodated by God) to our human nature. This is why Viret can write:

> He [God] is of too noble a heart and nature to exist without mercy and compassion. . . . And, because He is incapable of suffering in His divine nature, He took on ours in the person of His Son Jesus Christ, in which the Son of God suffered and endured alone more than all other men together.[26]

Viret even sees the supreme mark of God's love within

---

[24] Viret, *Instruction chrétienne*, Vol. II, p. 575.
[25] Analogy of proportion: a connection of resemblance, of partial identity between different realities previously submitted to comparison.
[26] Viret, *Instruction chrétienne*, Vol. II, p. 575.

the ignominy of Christ's death on the cross:

> This wound opens to us the very heart of God, as if we could clearly see it open before us, and all His inner being, in order that we might see and understand the fatherly love He bears us in His beloved Son.[27]

To end this chapter, we'll quote some of Pierre Viret's affirmations concerning the incarnation of the Son of God, the union of the two natures (divine and human) in a single divine Person, the Son of God made man:

> Paul particularly speaks of this divine nature when he says that He is "the image of the invisible God, the firstborn of every creature. For by Him were all things created, that are in heaven, and that are in earth, visible and invisible, whether they be thrones, or dominions, or principalities, or powers: all things were created by Him, and for Him: and He is before all things, and by Him all things consist" (Col. 1:15-17; Heb. 2:10; 4:12-13).
> Therefore he says in the chapter following: "in Him dwelleth all the fulness of the Godhead bodily," which is the same as if he'd said: "God dwells in other men by His Holy Spirit, kindling within them a new light and awakening in them new motions, but He dwells in Jesus Christ not only by His Spirit but also in His own essence and substance by a true union of the divine nature with the human in the same person" (Col. 2:9). For this term *bodily* means as much as if he said "substantially or personally, in His essence."[28]

Further on, when expounding the nature of the union of the divine and human natures within the single person of the Son of God made man, Viret, through his spokesman Philip,

---

[27] Viret, *Instruction chrétienne, Vol. II*, p. 502.
[28] Pierre Viret, *Jesus Christ: the Believer's Comfort and Joy* (Psalm 78 Ministries, Monticello, FL, 2019), p. 16.

recaptures the image employed by Athanasius (c. 298-373) of the union of the body and soul within the living person of man to attempt to render understandable the union of the divine and human natures in the person of the Son of God made man. Let's hear him:

> PHILIP: But we must consider this example here [taken from Athanasius] like the others we've already set forth in the matter of the Trinity [drawn mostly from the writings of Augustine], which is that it isn't so suitable that it doesn't have problems in some areas. Yet this doesn't hinder us from being able to provide a greater clarity to this point we're dealing with.

Viret explains:

> On this you must also note first that, if we can't fully comprehend how our soul is joined to and united with our body, a spiritual nature with a physical one, we shouldn't be surprised that we can't fully comprehend this inexpressible union that we're currently speaking of.[29]

Revealing here his perfect knowledge of the theological and metaphysical debates of the times of Maximus the Confessor (580-662) on monophysitism (a single soul) and monothelitism (a single will) and the necessity of affirming the existence of the fully human soul as well as the fully human will of Christ in order to preserve the full humanity of the Son of God in His incarnation,[30] Viret goes even further:

> But this serves us in the first place to show that the divine nature didn't replace the soul in Jesus Christ's body, who possessed a human and natural soul

---

[29] Viret, *Jesus Christ*, p. 51.
[30] The third Council of Constantinople of 680-681 condemned monothelitism, which denied the orthodox belief which confessed that Christ is endowed with "two wills, though not opposed to each other, but a human will submitted to the divine will."

belonging to Him just like other men; and likewise that Jesus Christ's human nature isn't merely like the dwelling place of the divine and as if the divine nature simply lodged there in order to assist it without being united to it in a personal union (just as various heretics formerly affirmed).

To the contrary, this shows us that the divine nature is so united to the human nature (by which I mean the entire man, body and soul) that, just like the soul and body are only one man and one person, composed of a spiritual and a physical nature, so also His divine and human nature are only one Jesus Christ, true God and true Man together, in such a way that His divinity remains in its entirety without being mixed or confused with His humanity any more than the soul is mixed or confused with the body; and likewise His humanity remains in its entirety in both body and soul.

We see here how Viret, in a language understandable by all, recaptures with an admirable exactness and balance the very formulations of the Council of Chalcedon (AD 451). And Philip concludes for Viret:

> Secondly, just as the soul is the chief part of a person, which bears and sustains the body and which has the main actions and gives power to the body itself to labor by the ways that are proper and inherent to it, so also the divine nature sustains the human in Jesus Christ, and provides it power and strength to accomplish the divine works which are done by it. This is why Christ said: "the flesh profiteth nothing. . . . it is the Spirit that quickeneth" or gives life (John 6:63). For the flesh (the human nature) wouldn't possess this divine and eternal nature by itself if it weren't communicated to it by the divine nature united with it, which works in it to accomplish divine works just like a human soul in its own way works in the human body to produce

natural works and actions.[31]

What a surprising refutation of the *docetist* temptation to which all of modernity has succumbed, the Gnostic temptation of valuing the intellect over the sentiments, the soul over the body, and mathematical science over the substantial forms of the created order. Within the sphere of theology, this manifests itself in the docetist temptation to overvalue the divinity of Christ at the expense of His humanity.

---

[31] Viret, *Jesus Christ*, pp. 51-52.

CHAPTER THREE

Understanding the Created World and History

If we desire to see how Pierre Viret's theology differs from that of his excellent friend and co-laborer in the ministry John Calvin, we must turn to a doctrine defended with great fortitude (and with certain differences) by both Viret and Calvin. This doctrine is creation, the established order instituted by God at the beginning, during the first week of the world. If, at the beginning of his *Institutes of the Christian Religion,* Calvin summarizes the knowledge necessary for man as the joint knowledge of himself and of God, Pierre Viret in a certain measure proceeds differently in his *Christian Instruction in the Law and the Gospel.* For him, to the knowledge of himself and of God he adds the knowledge of creation and history. This double knowledge, also illuminated as it is by the written Word of God, the Bible, speaks to us of the sustaining and providential working of the divinity. Anne-Marie Salgat, in her excellent thesis largely consecrated to Viret's theology, very clearly grasps this difference of emphasis in the theology of the two Reformers. Hear what she says:

> For Viret insisted, and in this he stands in the mainstream of Christianity, that the Lord is known to us most significantly through his revelation [*ad extra*], and not in his essence [*ad intra*]. This God, whom we acknowledge and love as the Father of Jesus Christ, has chosen to show himself to us in his works, in the realm of this world, nature and history, which faith understands as the loving product of his creative will

and upholding intelligence. In the rest of this chapter, it will be seen how exceedingly at home Viret found himself as he expounded the doctrines of creation and providence, sharpening up those theological insights which the New Testament writers, in direct line with the Old Testament prophets, had singled out from their experience as worthy of becoming tradition, a tradition all theologians antedating Galileo have received and transmitted in the context of a pre-scientific [we would say "theological" and "qualitative"] understanding of the universe.

Anne-Marie Salgat continues:

> Like Calvin, more than Luther therefore, Viret recognized the value of secular knowledge. Not unlike Zwingli, he marshaled all branches of sixteenth-century knowledge, its arts and sciences and philosophies, into the service of Reformed theology. In his writings on creation and providence, he placed Plato and Aristotle, Pliny, Plutarch and Ovid, Galen and Avicenna side by side with Moses, Solomon and David, Paul, Augustine and Jerome as expositors of the truth. He cited, in similarly enthusiastic but somewhat more guarded and critical appreciation, these classical authors whom the humanists had first hailed as their sources. And it was possible for him to do so because he was convinced of the Holy Spirit's universal inspiration and of the unity of all truth and knowledge.[1]

This is why nearly the entire second volume of his *Christian Instruction* of 1564 is dedicated to the study of creation and providence.[2] Viret writes:

---

[1] Anne-Marie Salgat, *Aspects of the Life and Theology of Pierre Viret (1511-1571)* (Union Theological Seminary, New York, 1972), pp. 137-138.
[2] This second volume of the 1564 edition is being republished by L'Age d'Homme. It will be contained in volumes III and IV of Pierre Viret, *Instruction chrétienne*, presented and annotated by Arthur-Louis Hofer (L'Age d'Homme, Lausanne).

> For this reason, in sending forth my *Christian Instruction,* which has already been printed in part, I have greatly augmented it, particularly on the matter of the creation of the world and of God's providence among all creatures, and especially toward man, particularly for two reasons.

These two reasons are:

(1) the reality of this general revelation of God, and
(2) the necessity of refuting the atheism of his time.

Concerning the first reason, Viret writes:

> The first, because the Spirit of God often sets forth for us in the Holy Scriptures this entire visible world [note, "visible" and not "mathematical"!] as a vast book of nature and true natural theology, and sets forth all the creatures as preachers and universal witnesses of God their Creator and of His works and glory.

Then he adds:

> Yet, despite this, there are very few who possess such eyes as are necessary to read this book, and who have ears suitable to hear the voice and understand the sermons of these natural preachers—indeed even among the wisest men who have made the most diligent study of nature and who are most advanced in the knowledge of natural things and in the liberal arts and all human philosophy.

Viret then explains the reasons for his prodigious undertaking aimed at revealing the hand of God in everything, both within the order of creation as well as within human history.

> And therefore I have truly desired to show by these conversations in this second volume, by all the

> creatures, and particularly in the consideration of the body and soul of man and in the creation and dignity and excellence of both of them, how not only the most unlearned and the most ignorant can and ought to consider the works of creation and profit from a consideration of them in order to learn through them to recognize God their Creator and His providence in all creatures (and particularly in themselves) and to honor and glorify Him as they ought; but also how the wisest men must make all science and all the knowledge they have of anything and all liberal arts and human philosophy serve this very same end—particularly natural philosophy [those who practice what we call "the sciences"] and the study of medicine.[3]

What Viret aims at here is nothing other than to apply the order given by the Apostle Paul: labor to bring every human thought captive to the obedience of Jesus Christ (2 Cor. 10:4-5).

But Viret pursues a second aim, which is a response to the "atheists" of his time, a scientific sect which excluded God and His Word from their science, a brotherhood which has become nearly universal today and a spirit which has, in a more or less large measure, infected many Christians as well. Let's hear Pierre Viret once again:

> The other cause which also moved me to deal with these matters so fully is atheism and those who make a profession of it, whom I just mentioned. For, since they despise and reject the testimonies that God has given of Himself in His Word and in His providence and His Church, and all things pertaining to salvation and the ultimate good of men, I truly desired to set forth a great part of the testimonies which all nature and this entire visible world renders us of all these things—and particularly within man, who is commonly called a little world—in order that these dogs and cunning beasts might be convinced, not only by the testimony

---

[3] Pierre Viret, *Instruction chrétienne*, Vol. II, pp. vi-vii.

of all the other creatures, but also by those which each of them carry within themselves, both of the reality of God and His providence, religion and divine justice, heaven and hell, the immortal nature of the soul, and a second life and a second death.

Viret is perfectly aware that these atheists are scarcely able to be convinced even by the best and sanest proofs drawn from the natural order. Thus he turns to the Christians who might be tempted to be seduced by this poisoned ideology:

> And, in order that it might not appear to many that I have labored in vain with regards to such persons who make a mockery of all remonstrances and corrections, I truly desire my readers to understand that it isn't mainly for them that I have labored in this work but for those who might be in danger of being seduced by them, in order that they might be better armed against the diabolical philosophy of these philosophers and hellish doctors who seek nothing but to misrepresent those of the true religion and to distort the study of the Holy Scriptures and those who believe its teaching.

Then Viret shows the harmony existing between the two books of God, the book of the Bible and the book of the created order and divine providence:

> And therefore within this volume I join the book of nature together with the book written with divine letters; and I unite natural philosophy and theology with its supernatural counterpart; and I show how the creatures and visible and physical things are pictures and illustrations of invisible and spiritual things; and how through the knowledge of the one we can mount up to the knowledge of the others—indeed, to God the Creator and the sovereign good of all.

Viret ends by affirming that he isn't trying to dabble in

the various sciences as a specialized practitioner, but only seeks to show how each human discipline can be understood and leads to the greater glory of Him who is its Author, God:

> For I'm not taking it upon myself to speak of the arts and sciences which belong to them as if I were making a profession of them, but only to show what their true use is, and how they can be employed for the honor of God, and how human sciences can assist the knowledge of divine science when they are applied to their true use as they ought to be.[4]

We have in this second volume a magisterial apologetic response to those—and the entirety of modernity could be included here—who read the book of nature and history while excluding Him who is their Creator, sovereign Meaning, and Providence. Anne-Marie Salgat puts it very well:

> Thus it is clear that, since unaided observation of and inquiry into nature can lead man to such false (because so varied) opinions about the nature of God, men must rely on God's revelation of himself: the Savior and Redeemer in Jesus Christ, his Son.[5]

Viret here is certainly thinking of the Epicureans and Stoics who exclude the true God from history and nature. The first do so by denying Him; the second by subjecting Him to the absolute reign of the laws of nature.

We'll end by quoting two excerpts from this divine Word which led Viret every step in his immense enterprise by which he sought to understand the world, both created and fallen, by the light of heavenly realities, realities of which the concrete and physical forms of the world, ordained and governed by God, testify in such an eloquent way:

---

[4] Viret, *Instruction chrétienne, Vol. II*, pp. vii-viii.
[5] Salgat, *Aspects of the Life and Theology of Pierre Viret*, p. 139.

> Our Father which art in heaven,
> Hallowed be thy name.
> Thy kingdom come.
> Thy will be done
> In earth, as it is in heaven!
>
> Matthew 6:9-10

This work of the sanctification of men and the world is echoed in the words of the psalmist:

> I will hear what God the Lord will speak: for he will speak peace unto his people, and to his saints: but let them not turn again to folly. Surely his salvation is nigh them that fear him; that glory may dwell in our land. Mercy and truth are met together; righteousness and peace have kissed each other. Truth shall spring out of the earth; and righteousness shall look down from heaven. Yea, the Lord shall give that which is good; and our land shall yield her increase. Righteousness shall go before him; and shall set us in the way of his steps.
>
> Psalm 85:8-13

CHAPTER FOUR

Assessing Viret's Theology: John Calvin in the light of Pierre Viret

What value should we place on Viret's theology? As we've seen, we have two studies on his theology: the first is that of Georges Bavaud, a Vaudois Roman Catholic canon who dedicated the majority of his studies to examine the thought of our Reformer. The second is that of Anne-Marie Salgat, who dedicated a doctoral thesis to him. Georges Bavaud sees Viret through his Roman lenses; Anne Marie Salgat from a rather liberal background. Both show the liveliest admiration for the work of Pierre Viret as well as a vast understanding of his thought. The majority of historians who have examined his life and work have considered him as a rather modest disciple of John Calvin, developing his theology under the shadow of the Genevan Reformer. It's true that on many sides, and on essential matters, their theology is in agreement.

But to consider the matter more closely, the historical perspective of Viret as a disciple of Calvin is scarcely in keeping with the facts. We must note that the first manifestations of Pierre Viret's thought date from his return to Orbe in 1531, five years before the first edition of Calvin's *Institutes of the Christian Religion* at Basel. The first written expressions of Viret's thought date from the Lausanne Disputation held in the cathedral of that city in the beginning of October 1536. It was during this dispute that John Calvin made his entrance onto the scene of public theological debates. But during this meeting it was Pierre Viret who, under the very active directorship of William Farel, played the vital role. In the detailed records of this disputation we can clearly see to what point Viret's thought had already been truly formed and consolidated.

The second part of his life, the thirty-five years spanning from 1536 to his death in 1571, reveal and provide opportunities for a constant enrichment and a great strengthening of his thought. This thought became vaster, more balanced, and more exact in its formulation and wording but, above all, it became enormously diversified in its ever increasing and more precise application to the multiple and various aspects of men's thought and action. As the years passed, nothing seemed able to escape Viret's intellectual and spiritual appetite, an approach which sought with astonishing persistence to submit all things—both in nature and history—to the beneficent and life-giving authority of the Word of God.

Even though it would be impossible, in my opinion, to establish any fundamental opposition between the thought of these two friends, colleagues, and co-laborers throughout the many years passed in a mutual Christian battle, yet I believe it would be useful to note a few contrasts between these magisterial works in order to better appreciate the complementary—and occasionally quite diverse—nature of their approaches to the task of theologian. Thus let's quickly examine a few distinctive traits which characterize the labor and writings of these two most admirable men of God, Pierre Viret and John Calvin.

1) The majority of Calvin's work was originally written in the international academic language of the era: Latin. The vast majority of Viret's works were written in French.

2) Both Calvin's Latin and French works were written with a great eloquence in a splendid and at times even sublime prose. Viret wrote in a more popular, easy-going, and even spoken style, most often in the form of a conversation.

3) Viret, contrary to Calvin, didn't seek to reach an educated audience alone, but sought to connect with the reading public among the people.[1] The method of literary conversations that he employed gave his writings a certain similarity to the

---

[1] Indeed, it was the very "popular" nature of his writings which rendered the survival of Viret's works so precarious because they were read and reread until the books fell to pieces.

scholastic disciplines. Each subject studied is thus, through a conversation, approached from various aspects and from different angles. It is only after long exchanges that the reader reaches a fully developed formulation of the truth. Calvin's method is more logically direct, more deductive. Viret doesn't stop at a single source, the Bible, but makes use of partial truths which convey the water to his theological, philosophical, evangelical, and apologetic mill. It is thus within the culture of his time as well as within the entire classical heritage of western civilization that Viret draws the materials from which his eminently Christian thought is constructed.

4) Calvin has a deductive and direct style of thought and writing, drawing logical consequences from his biblical premises with the greatest clarity. Viret, by contrast, is attached to a more extensive discourse united to the conversational format of the majority of his works. As Dominique Troilo so aptly stated, "If Calvin's writing is like an arrow that unswervingly strikes its target in an unanswerable manner, for Viret, the picture would instead be that of a lasso which carefully and meticulously encircles its reader through a vast variety of arguments."

5) It's clear that Calvin maintained a very clean and clear distinction between truth and error, as Bertrand Rickenbacher puts it, going, like an arrow, straight to the point and leaving scarcely any alternative for his reader between accepting or refusing his powerfully logical and sharply concise argument. Viret, however, works in another way. Before arriving at his conclusions (which are in general just as unanswerable as Calvin's), his use of a conversation provides his readers a chance to breathe and to carefully consider the various viewpoints on a particular question before arriving at a conclusion for themselves.

6) Calvin thus succeeded in convincing his reader by arguments from which there was no escape. Viret, on the other hand, sought to gradually persuade his audience of the reasonable—and biblical—nature of his words. He almost always worked through friendly discussions between typical people defending various points of view.

7) Thus Calvin opened the way for the clarity and conciseness of French prose. In one sense he was one of the precursors of classical clarity and precision. We could, at least in part, make the thought of Calvin dependent on that of a Plato (Jean Boisset) or even a Duns Scotus (Francois Wendel). He proceeds completely differently than Viret's constantly recapitulative style. Viret seeks to make the flow of his thought more and more capable of capturing the matter examined by stressing each point with a haunting repetition which, at its foundation, has a rather Hebraic character. Through conversation he manages to express different viewpoints on a particular subject, thus allowing his reader to grasp every aspect of the reality under his attention. In contrast to Calvin's style, this way of thinking and writing draws its roots from more ancient forms of expression—Hebraic with regard to the repetitions, scholastic and platonic with regard to the conversations, and Aristotelian with regard to his constant concern for realism. Viret's conversations, by their measured advancement to the truth through the friendly discussion of very different points of view, presents us with a popularized form of the scholastic method with its well-regulated stages of affirmation, refutation, confirmation, and final synthesis.

8) Calvin's clearly deductive method occasionally led to conclusions beyond what could legitimately be drawn from the biblical data. Viret, by contrast, through the conversational method, is gradually led to express his thought that, in one way, is often ultimately more biblically exact and balanced than his colleague and Genevan friend. In this Viret particularly resembles the Zurich Reformer Heinrich Bullinger, who (with great tact) often exercised a moderating influence on his younger colleague, John Calvin. Bullinger occasionally encouraged Calvin to moderate his at times extreme expressions in these words: "The fathers never expressed it in that way." Viret's theological style is thus often characterized by an equilibrium, a sense of balance, moderation, and a most remarkable exactness—certainly not mathematical, but biblical. Here a meticulous and detailed comparative study of the theological styles of Viret and Calvin would

be truly revealing.

9) This leads us to a comparison of the perception of the natural world according to Calvin and Viret. Both believed in the divine origin of creation as it is described in the first two chapters of Genesis and also elsewhere in the Bible; both defended God's sovereign ordinance of every aspect of the creation in six days; both believed that the order of the cosmos, created stable from the beginning, is constantly upheld in its proper order by God through His powerful Word; both believed providence to be the governing force of history; both were certain that the sighs and groans of creation would end at the last day, at the removal of the corrupted world and the renewal of all things; finally, both believed in the miraculous working of God even within the established order of the universe.

Thus is there any difference between how these two grand theologians perceived the order of nature?

Calvin, once again, by his manner of thinking, looked toward the future, toward the new classical and scientific world already on the horizon of European civilization, a culture in which mathematical and experimental science would determine the understanding that we would possess of the universe. His worldview was a stranger to that of the Middle Ages and, in a certain measure, to that of antiquity. Calvin had scarcely any sympathy for a *moral* conception of the natural order such as is found in Aesop's fables, in the Fabliau, and in the bestiaries of the Middle Ages. According to Calvin, the moral order of men is entirely distinct from the purely natural—zoological and biological—order of animal and vegetable life.

For Viret, on the other hand, every aspect of creation is full of moral and spiritual significance. Though he certainly didn't espouse a rationalist and allegorically moralizing mode of thought—such as is found in Philo of Alexandria, Origen, Augustine, or Gregory the Great—however his thought was instead similar to the analogical mode of the parables and images of the Bible. Thus Viret readily speaks of the life of all types of animals—terrestrial, aquatic, and birds of the air. From their formation and habits he draws lessons relating both to the life of men as well as moral and theological lessons, both natural and spiritual.

From this viewpoint, Viret is rather a medieval thinker who has strayed into the beginnings of modernity. By contrast, Calvin's reluctance to perceive the moral sense of nature in the habits of the species below man contains the premonitions of the new vision which was knocking at the door of the sixteenth century. For, as regards Modernity, the subhuman world—and, more and more, the human world itself—contains no more than a functional, technical, utilitarian significance. Of course, for him—though to a lesser degree than Calvin—this new "scientific" way of looking at reality also tended to reveal the great glory of the Creator. However, Viret himself is much more interested in the moral and spiritual wisdom present in the order created by God than was Calvin, his great friend, ministerial colleague, and fellow-soldier.

Let's draw up a brief contrast between the two spiritual families represented by John Calvin and Pierre Viret.

A) We are told that violent men take the Kingdom of God by force, while the meek will inherit the earth. Among Christian figures such as the Apostle Paul, Athanasius, Maximus the Confessor, John Wycliffe, Martin Luther, William Farel, J. Gresham Machen, Rousas J. Rushdoony, or Pierre Courthial—and among these lights John Calvin assumes an eminent place—we find ourselves in the company of these "violent men." They are those who through their thoughts and acts reveal the actualization, the prophetic emergence of the Kingdom of God among us. This victory of the Kingdom in time is always preceded by the manifestation, in time and Christian history, of the "birth pains" of the Church. This is the actualization, within time and space, of the definitive destruction of the works of the devil accomplished once for all by Jesus Christ in His definitive victorious death on the cross of Golgotha. But it is through such men—these "violent" men—that the reign of God advances on the earth.

B) Yet another family of Christians exists who are the meek and humble, those who will inherit the earth. It is here that we find, among others, Christians such as the Apostle John, Irenaeus of Lyons, Gregory of Nazianzus, Ephraim the Syrian, and Aphrahat the Persian Sage; it's in this company that we must place Heinrich Bullinger and Pierre Viret, the latter of whom was called *the Angel of the Reformation*. By their meekness, their balanced gentleness, and their modesty, they reveal the spirit of the new heavens and the new earth, a time and place where all tears will be wiped away, where righteousness will dwell, and where there will be no more sorrow.

The contrast that we've laid out in a great measure allows us to explain the immense renown of John Calvin and the astonishing oblivion which was to be the fate of Pierre Viret, his comrade of so many battles for God and His Kingdom.

This contrast is revealed in the most visible way in the very titles of their two respective masterpieces: *Institutes of the Christian Religion* for Calvin and *Christian Instruction in the Doctrine of the Law and the Gospel* for Viret. To the title of this last masterful work, the subtitle must be added:

> *Christian Instruction in the Doctrine of the Law and the Gospel in true Christian philosophy and theology, both natural and supernatural, and in the contemplation of the temple and the images and works of the providence of God through the entire universe; and in the history of the creation and fall and restoration of mankind*[2]

The verbose character of Viret's title offers a striking contrast to the brilliant conciseness of Calvin's masterful work. But there is more here than a simple formal difference. For Calvin his *Institutes*—which is a legal expression; consider the *Institutes*

---

[2] You can see in the Viretian expression: "Creation, fall, and restoration of humankind" the distant premonition of the well-known expression of Abraham Kuyper (1837-1920) formulated by him to succinctly express the full scope of the work of God: "Creation, fall, redemption."

of Justinian or Gracian—represent a *Summa,* a sum or summary of the entire Christian religion. His purpose is explicitly religious and theological.

Matters are different for Viret. Calvin, within the very title of his *Institutes,* insists on the Gospel, speaking as he does of the *Christian Religion,* thus immediately distinguishing between the New and the Old Covenant, the Gospel and the Law. Viret, on the other hand, is much more complete. For, as we've seen, we find even within the very title of his work the Christian character of his *Christian Instruction,* for the Christian doctrine itself being presented there clearly and most explicitly consists of an Old Covenant strictly united to a New Covenant.

For, for Viret, the summary (*summa*) of the Christian religion doesn't consist of the Gospel alone or even less of the Law alone, but of the unity of the Law and the Gospel, an inseparable union maintained by the catholic—that is, *complete*—character of the revelation of God, the entirety of the Scriptures: *Tota Scriptura.* For him, as for the seer of the Revelation, "the testimony of Jesus is the spirit of prophecy" (Rev. 19:10).

The teaching of Viret resembles a marvelous sculpture of a capital placed atop a column in the abbey of Vezelay and entitled *The Mystic Mill.* On one side Moses is seen symbolically pouring grain (the Old Covenant) into a mill (the sacrificial work of Christ). And, on the other side, Paul is seen gathering the wheat (ground by the cross) of the Gospel. For Viret affirms in his very title that both the Law and the Gospel form the two inseparable facets of the Message of God.

We must also note that in the title of his masterful work Viret doesn't limit himself, as Calvin does, to Christian theology alone, but speaks explicitly of a true philosophy and theology, together holding the unity of true knowledge, both natural and supernatural. In this way he preserves the harmony existing between the first creation—a creation good but fallen—and its restoration in the second, in which all righteousness will dwell throughout eternity.

Thus Viret includes in his *Christian Instruction* the

totality of the created order as well as the totality of the new creation, a universe (cosmos, world) redeemed and restored by the redemptive work of the Son of God in which all the promises of the Old Covenant are fulfilled. And, in the beginning of his work, Viret adds an element which isn't found in Calvin's *Institutes:* "the contemplation of the temple [creation] and the images [the physical forms, the creatures] and the works of the providence of God [revealing itself through history and culture] through the entire universe."

Viret thus includes in the very *summary* of his *Christian Instruction* his foundation: (1) a theological history of the Bible and (2) a history of creation, the fall, and the restoration of humanity. In passing, we should note here that the eloquent expression of Abraham Kuyper: "Creation, fall, redemption" finds its origin in the final words of the complete title of Viret's *Christian Instruction.*

Conclusion

As we've seen, one of Viret's most important theological successes was to give the providence of God its full importance, both concerning creation as well as history, in the context of biblical Revelation, and even within the divine creation. Thus, as I sought to show in my little book *Pierre Viret: a Forgotten Giant of the Reformation,* a majestic vision of the grandeur of the historical, redemptive, and creative work of God led our Vaudois Reformer to discover that Scripture contains this same divine Word (here inscripturated) which is also found in the natural, creational order. This Word, the Bible, is the same Logos which forms, upholds, and restores the fallen order of the world. Thus, for Viret, it is truly Scripture alone that reveals the meaning that God has given to all things—which explains his passion to understand and teach even the very least of God's commandments—and thus all creational and providential reality must also conceal and possess the wisdom of a meaning ordained by God Himself.

Even more, if the Gospel finds its foundation in the written

Scriptures of God, it equally receives an unsuspected support from even the least aspect of created and providential reality. Thus for Viret, and for those who share his fully divine and fully creational vision of reality—such as Tyconius, John Wycliffe, Lancelot Andrewes, James Ussher, Johann Georg Hamann, Friedrich Julius Stahl, Groen van Prinsterer, J. Gresham Machen, Hendrik Stoker, Rousas John Rushdoony, Pierre Courthial, and Douglas Kelly—the entirety of Scripture illuminates reality. But, conversely as well, the entirety of reality perceived by the light of the divine Word speaks of the immutable wisdom, justice, goodness, and peace of the thrice holy God, truths infallibly expressed in the Bible.

We'll conclude with an example. In light of what we've described, a light in which the special and general revelation of God are mutually supportive, it is clear that the battle led by J. Gresham Machen (1881-1937) to crush the pseudo-scientific modern criticism of the New Testament (and its offspring, historicism) is fully justified. For it was by strenuously laboring as a most exact and precise historian that Machen destroyed the fallacious arguments of his adversaries and critics of the Bible. He did this not by the power of (perfectly exact) logical deductions drawn from the affirmations of the special revelation of God on the topic of His own infallibility (as did his predecessor at Princeton, Benjamin Warfield), but through the facts of the history of salvation itself. For, contrary to the modern idea we possess of the nature of our world (a conception fabricated by the theories of a dualist and Gnostic science), the created world, the historic world—a true world, ordained and governed by God—cannot be separated, by the arbitrary critical hypotheses of man, from this divine, inspired, written, and infallible Word, the Bible. For, let us truly remember:

*What God has joined together, let no man have
the audacity to put asunder!*

Amen!

CHAPTER FIVE

Man as the Image of God According to Pierre Viret: A Reading by Douglas Kelly

Foreword[1]

The presentation that I've come to share with you this evening is given, not on the elite triumvirate which was William Farel, Pierre Viret, and John Calvin (to maintain the order of their appearance on the scene of the Reformation), but on a more diverse trio, part old and part modern: Pierre Viret, of course; his Calvinist reader from the other side of the Atlantic, professor Douglas F. Kelly from the Reformed Theological Seminary in Charlotte, North Carolina; and my own modest person. I have attempted, through Douglas Kelly's study, to show what a modern Reformed reading can be from this crowning point of Christian theology: the image of God in man.

But to these three musketeers of the Word we must obviously add a fourth: our eldest, he who has opened for us all the path of Viretian studies. I speak here, as you've already realized, of the scholarly editor of the works of Pierre Viret who has shown us the honor of joining us this evening, pastor Arthur-Louis Hofer. It is by quoting him that we will begin this study.

Introduction

At the end of the third volume of Pierre Viret's *Instruction chrétienne*, to which we here desire to render homage, Arthur-Louis Hofer writes:

---

[1] This chapter was originally presented as a lecture to the Association Pierre Viret in Lausanne on November 25, 2015.

> The third volume of this new edition masterfully reveals why Viret's sermons enjoyed such a success. As expressions of his oratorical skill, they join "the book of nature with the written book of divine letters." Bible in hand, his sermons bind nature and man to God their Creator. Within this book the Reformer forever asserts his own personality alongside Farel and Calvin, three friends, the elite Triumvirate.[2]

In fact, this third volume (as well as the first part of the fourth) shows us—which we see from the Reformer's very first works—that for Pierre Viret, in the lavish detail of creation, even the most modest of the works of God reveal the glory and supreme wisdom of the Creator. In his *Métamorphose chrétienne* of 1561 (an enlarged republication of his *Dialogues du désordre* of 1545), we read a beautiful expression of a thought which always marked his writings:

> For this world in which we live, what is it but the very temple of God, a temple in which he represents and manifests himself to us? And all his creatures, what are they but the most vivid images of himself? What is the whole framework of this visible world but a shop in which God, that incomparable artisan, has displayed his works to make us discover, by his craftsmanship, what manner of worker he is and in what admiration and reverence we should hold him? And to realize this we need not leave this garden to seek such signs abroad. Let us simply consider the immense variety of images of his power, wisdom and goodness God has set here before our eyes. For we have seen as many of these signs as we have observed plants, grasses, leaves and flowers, and these more vivid and true to life than all the images the priests have strewn about their temples. For in these we find neither life, nor fragrance, nor profit, nor usefulness of any kind; nor

---
[2] Pierre Viret, *Instruction chrétienne en la Loi et l'Évangile, Tome III* (L'Age d'Homme, Lausanne, 2013), p. 926.

do they contain anything which could remind us of God and speak to us of his gifts and graces.³

This evening, with the assistance of a recent study (as of yet unpublished)⁴ by Douglas Kelly, professor of systematic theology at the Reformed Theological Seminary in Charlotte, we'll take a short summary glance over the way (certainly unusual for the classical Reformed crowd, but yet quite orthodox) in which Pierre Viret considers the entire man, body and soul, as a faithful image—though certainly neither exhaustive nor univocal—of the only God, the Father, Son, and Holy Spirit, to whom be honor, glory, and power forever and ever. Amen.

Our study will consist of three parts, followed by a conclusion:

1. Two views of the world.
2. The thought of the Reformers concerning the image of God.
3. The image of God according to Pierre Viret.
Conclusion.

1. Two Views of the World

Before beginning an examination of the positions of various Reformed theologians concerning the nature of the image of God in man, Douglas Kelly contrasts the cosmological foundations—the worldview of the universe—of these former Reformed theologians with those that we are so familiar with today. For, through the universal application of this new model of the world by the spirit of the Enlightenment which is that of the entire world today, we are all heirs of this new science which

---

³ Pierre Viret, *Métamorphose chrétienne, faite par dialogues* (Jacques Bres, Geneva, 1561), pp. 2-3. Quoted in Jean-Marc Berthoud, *Pierre Viret: a Forgotten Giant of the Reformation* (Zurich Publishing, Tallahassee, FL, 2010), p. 58.

⁴ *Translator's note:* Douglas Kelly's study "Creation, Mankind, and the Image of God" has since been published in Matthew Barrett, ed., *Reformation Theology: a Systematic Summary* (Crossway, Wheaton, IL, 2017). Page numbers corresponding to this work have been attached to the quotations derived from this previously-unpublished study.

began its conquering flight at the beginning of the seventeenth century. I'll quote Douglas Kelly:

> Before we survey the Reformers' teaching on the divine image in humankind, we must briefly consider the massive intellectual gap between their confidence in the plain meaning of Holy Scripture and the post-Enlightenment rejection of its authority as regards its historical and scientific truth claims.[5]

Kelly explains:

> The eighteenth-century Enlightenment (especially in its later phases) placed the powers of human reason above the divine revelation [first of all in what concerned the sphere of physical science] in such a way that it rejected much of the biblical worldview and replaced it with current theories of those who were at that time in the intellectual vanguard.[6]

Douglas Kelly continues:

> For that reason, particularly with the development of deism (which excluded God's intervention in the natural world), many outright rejected the miraculous and especially the biblical accounts of divine creation within the space of six days only a few thousand years ago.

He adds:

> Those [Christians] who felt that they needed to come to terms with these early forms of what would later be called "secularism" [i.e., cosmological atheism]

---

[5] Douglas Kelly, "Creation, Mankind, and the Image of God," in Matthew Barrett, ed., *Reformation Theology: a Systematic Summary* (Crossway, Wheaton, IL, 2017), p. 289.
[6] This rejection particularly concerns the biblical view of the world but, in a certain measure, also that of all culture preceding the appearance of the new mathematical-experimental sciences at the beginning of the seventeenth century.

were faced with the hard problem of proposed reinterpretations of miracles and divine creation. The two worldviews were incompatible: belief in divine intervention and belief in secularism (also known as naturalism) rendered contrary accounts of the meaning of nature in general and the significance of mankind in particular.[7]

After this introduction, I'll now move on to the second point of Professor Kelly's exposition.

2. THE TEACHING OF THE REFORMERS CONCERNING THE IMAGE OF GOD

Turning to the Reformers and their view of reality, Douglas Kelly writes:

> Any serious reading of the Reformers will show that they developed their doctrine on the basis of the traditional biblical worldview with its commitment to God's intervention into the natural realm and his accurate account of it in Holy Scripture. Of course, Luther, Calvin, and the other Reformers were well aware of ancient forms of secularist explanations of the cosmos, such as the atomic theories of Democritus and Lucretius, which had no recourse to God, nor to any miracles he might perform in the world.[8]

Pierre Viret, for his part, dreaded the increasing spread (even in his day) of this atheistic ideology of the "Epicurean"[9] atomic scientists, a worldview which very suddenly came to take an unsuspected importance and far-reaching range with the birth of the new sciences. According to him, this atheistic offensive represented for the Reformation (and for Christianity

---

[7] Kelly, "Creation, Mankind, and the Image of God" in *Reformation Theology*, p. 289.
[8] Kelly, "Creation, Mankind, and the Image of God," pp. 289-290.
[9] Derived from the use of the quite common (particularly with Calvin) expression of the "Epicurean swine" to characterize the partisans of this rejection of God within nature and history.

itself) a much more formidable danger than all the (very real!) errors of Roman Catholicism. Kelly concludes:

> But [the Reformers] wrote off these atheistic theories and believed that with the truth of the Scriptures, they were standing in the divinely revealed light by which alone they could make sense of nature and mankind.[10]

Kelly then examines the position of several Reformed and Lutheran theologians on the character and nature of the image of God in man. He thus quickly reviews the positions of Luther and Melanchthon, Zwingli and Bullinger, Calvin, Tyndale, Capito, and John Knox, as well as also probing a few Reformed confessions of faith. When considering Luther and Calvin's commentaries on Genesis and Paul's epistle to the Romans, Douglas Kelly arrives at the following conclusions:

1.   Both taught the truth of a direct creation by God of all things in six days, events which occurred only a few thousand years ago.
2.   They equally taught that Adam was the head of the entire human race. He was the very image of God, and both this image as well as its present state of sin were transmitted to the entirety of humankind—with, of course, the exception of Christ, who alone was conceived and born without sin.
3.   It was impossible for the Reformers to accept that the creational attributes of God could in any way be transferred to any sort of a natural, evolutionary process.
4.   Their teaching clearly reflected that of their predecessors, both the patristic and scholastic doctors, whose successors they were.

Then Kelly explains the fully classical position of these Reformed theologians concerning the image of God in man. This is what he writes on the thought of Calvin (the great friend

---

[10] Kelly, "Creation, Mankind, and the Image of God," p. 290.

and colleague of Viret) on man, the image of God:

> Calvin, the magisterial biblical expositor and theologian, held that as far as man is concerned, "the proper seat of his [i.e., God's] image is in the soul." Calvin understood "soul" and "spirit" to be essentially the same and viewed it as "separable from the body."[11]

Kelly explains Calvin's thought:

> [Calvin writes:] "Man was created therefore in the image of God, and in him the Creator was pleased to behold as in a mirror His own glory." But at the same time, Calvin insisted that the image is *internal* to man. "The likeness must be within, in himself. It must be something which is not external to him, but is properly the internal good of the soul."[12]

Kelly again quotes Calvin:

> "From this we infer that, to begin with, God's image was visible in the light of the mind, in the uprightness of the heart, and in the soundness of all the parts."

Calvin continues:

> Now we see how Christ [in his humanity] is the most perfect image of God; if we are conformed to it, we are so restored that with true piety, righteousness, purity, and intelligence we bear God's image.[13]

Kelly ends his summary of the position espoused by John Calvin on the image of God in man with these words:

> Calvin did not totally deny that some sparkling of

---

[11] Kelly, "Creation, Mankind, and the Image of God," p. 295.
[12] Kelly, "Creation, Mankind, and the Image of God," p. 296.
[13] Kelly, "Creation, Mankind, and the Image of God," p. 297.

God's image shone in man's body or that dominion over the rest of the created order was connected to it, but he did not lay emphasis on either of these two aspects, instead focusing on the spiritual: "The glory of God peculiarly shines forth in human nature where the mind, will, and all the senses, represent the divine order."[14]

3. The Image of God according to Pierre Viret

It's striking to note that Douglas Kelly spends as much time describing Pierre Viret's thought on the image of God as he gives to John Calvin himself. To do this he draws from the 337 pages of the recently republished third volume of Pierre Viret's *Instruction chrétienne*.[15] I'll begin by quoting Kelly:

> Pierre Viret of Lausanne was a close colleague of Calvin and frequent correspondent, and at one time he even served as Calvin's assistant in Geneva. Viret wrote the fullest and perhaps the most interesting account of man's creation in the image of God of any leader of the sixteenth-century Reformation. In the third volume of his works (published in French in 2013), Viret devoted almost 350 pages to various aspects of man's creation in the image of God.[16]

Let's follow the assessment that Professor Kelly gives of this immense study that Pierre Viret devotes to the entire man, body and soul together, as the image of God. Kelly remarks that Viret dedicates the greatest part of his treatise to a very detailed consideration of "The image and the grandeur and infinity of God in this visible world,"[17] after which he more specifically turns his attention to what he calls "The external edifice of the

---

[14] Kelly, "Creation, Mankind, and the Image of God," p. 297.
[15] Pages 405 to 742.
[16] Kelly, "Creation, Mankind, and the Image of God," pp. 298-299.
[17] Pierre Viret, *Instruction chrétienne, Tome III*, p. 405. This is the title of the second dialogue.

human body" as the image of God.[18]

> In this Viret differs from the main trend of Reformed tradition, both of his contemporaries of the sixteenth century as well as of the view of the image of God in man which would become that of the majority of confessional Reformed theologians of the following centuries.[19]

Kelly continues:

> Much of [Viret's] interest in the body was because the Lord planned it to be a worthy temple for the incarnation of his Son. As though this were a manual of gross anatomy, Viret covered such parts of the body as ligaments, cartilages, and nerves. He listed man's two feet and legs as enabling him to stand upright and his hands as "the cause of science and wisdom."[20]

It would be worthwhile to pause a moment to hear Pierre Viret's actual words:

> Contrary to [the animals], man can't walk or do anything skillfully while lying down or leaning on the ground like the beasts; but when he is standing or seated, he can perform all his works quite easily. For, just as God gave him two legs and two feet to hold him up and carry him wherever he wants to go, so also He gave him two arms and two hands to perform all the works he desires to accomplish. Therefore Aristotle rightly calls the hand "the instrument of instruments." For there is no member of the entire body, or any instrument at all, which performs more works or a

---

[18] This is the title of the twelfth dialogue. The entire first part of the (forthcoming) fourth volume of this republication Viret dedicates, in a dazzlingly beautiful way, to the theme of "the internal edifice of the human body."
[19] Douglas Kelly, "Creation, Mankind, and the Image of God," unpublished paper.
[20] Kelly, "Creation, Mankind, and the Image of God," in Matthew Barrett, ed., *Reformation Theology*, p. 299.

greater variety of them. For this is the instrument that makes all others and which puts them all to work, as we see by experience. And, because man is the only creature among all the animals who is capable of arts and skilled labor and the only one who knows how to labor in these fields, God gave him alone this instrument to perform these things.[21]

Thus for Viret the hand is a mark of the image of God in man, and it is therefore in no way inappropriate to speak—in an analogical way, of course, but in any case in a quite exact manner (as the Bible so often does)—of the hand of God as the instrument of His power, both intelligent and effective.

Pierre Viret continues:

We also see that man knows how to accomplish every work by the use of his hands. And what work of God exists that he hasn't attempted to reproduce as if he were a little god on earth who attempted to create another visible world within this world created by God?[22]

This, it seems to me, is a prophetic statement pointing to the project of a "new world" such as was soon to be imagined by the scientific utopias of such thinkers as Francis Bacon and René Descartes, a world created by human artifice issuing from the new Science and the technologies it would produce, this *technocosmos*—to use Jan Marejko's word—in which we live today.

But Viret also sees the works issuing from the human hand in a much more positive way. Let's hear what he says:

For if we consider men's sciences, arts, and occupations, and the excellent works that they create through the use of their hands, who wouldn't stand and marvel? We could truly agree with the statement of those

---

[21] Pierre Viret, *Instruction chrétienne, Tome III*, pp. 494-495.
[22] Viret, *Instruction chrétienne, Tome III*, p. 495.

who say that *the hand is the source of science and wisdom*. For if it didn't write letters and draw figures and if it didn't make the instruments required and necessary for all sciences and occupations, we could never teach or learn anything at all.

Nathaniel—the disciple of Philip his teacher in these conversations in *Instruction chrétienne*—here poses the question: shouldn't man then be considered "like a second creator?", a question which gives rise to a very instructive response from Philip—the character who represents the Reformed teacher, in fact the position of Viret himself—on the difference between human works and God's works. Let's hear the master's response:

> PHILIP: It is just as you say. But there is a vast difference between the works of men and those of God, particularly in three points: in matter, form, and life (and everything it bears with it).[23]
>
> For, first, man can't labor without matter or material, and he can't find this in himself as God did, who created everything out of nothing and who created being out of what didn't exist (Rom. 4:17). But man works in a completely different way. For he can't create anything out of nothing, but instead he is required to first possess the material he desires to use in his work, which he merely gives form to.
>
> Second, you must also note that he can't give any form to anything unless he first has a model in the works of God. For, even though he can imagine very strange things that he's never seen an example similar to in the entirety of nature or among any of the creatures, yet he can't imagine anything so new or so strange that it doesn't already exist in some way or

---

[23] We see here the ease with which Viret appropriately and suitably employs Aristotelian vocabulary while bringing to it a biblical fullness, for to Aristotle's *matter* and *form* Viret adds *life*. We can also see the same with the ideas drawn from the platonic tradition which he always reshapes to a biblical perspective. In this he parallels the practice of the Church fathers, who took the good from all literary sources, taking these Egyptian treasures captive to the obedience of Christ.

in some model in God's works in various creatures. For he takes various pieces from various things, which he then masses together in an attempt to reproduce something quite new.[24]

This is even true concerning the strange beasts of Scripture, in particular those in Daniel and above all in Revelation, monstrous figures which are made up of a bizarre collection of various created forms. We also find the same in some painters who were contemporaries of Viret, such as Jerome Bosch in particular and also at times in the works of Pierre Breugel the Elder.

On the third point, Philip explains to Nathaniel that the most beautiful artistic expressions have never possessed either life or movement or living souls. Let's listen to him develop this last point which distinguishes—in the most beautifully scholastic manner—man's works from those of God.

> But yet there is neither soul, life, feeling, movement, sense or understanding, nor reason or intelligence even in the most beautiful idol or in the most beautiful god that all the most excellent painters and sculptors could ever create or reproduce. For they can't even give their creations as much life as a turnip or an onion possesses, or some other herb or plant, or as much movement or feeling or ingenuity as a fly or an ant possesses, or the least worm that crawls on the earth.[25]

Douglas Kelly continues by noting the prodigious theological and anatomical interest Viret shows by scrutinizing every part of human anatomy to find various aspects of the image of God in man everywhere within it.

> He briefly mentioned the sexual organs, the stomach, and the womb for the passing on and nourishment of

---

[24] Viret, *Instruction chrétienne*, Tome III, p. 495.
[25] Viret, *Instruction chrétienne*, Tome III, pp. 497-498.

physical life. He dealt with the flesh, with muscles, and with glands. He discussed the providence of God in forming women's breasts (and the glands that sustain them). He talked about the usefulness of one's hair. He stated how physical beauty is joined to the utility and commodity of the human body.[26]

These remarks on the beauty of the human body sharply contrast with those which (at times so denigrating to this subject) are found in the writings of his colleague and friend John Calvin, who was otherwise so enamored with the beauty of art, Scripture, and that of the world, the "theater of God's glory."[27] Let's hear Pierre Viret again as he expresses himself through Philip his spokesman:

> What I'm trying to say is that, because God chose to give man a body with a beauty far surpassing that of any of the other creatures, He also willed that this beauty appear in all parts of it. For, first, you see that this body wasn't formed either to fly in the air like the birds or to crawl on the earth and slither and drag itself along on its stomach like the reptiles, or to walk on four feet like the beasts of the earth that walk like this. Nor was man made with his head leaning down toward the earth like these are, but instead to stand and walk upright, with his head elevated and raised up toward heaven (as we already mentioned previously), in order that he might learn even from the formation of his body that his true origin and birth come from a much higher place than the earth and other corruptible elements—that is, from heaven.[28]

I'll also quote a passage in which Pierre Viret expresses

---

[26] Douglas Kelly, "Creation, Mankind, and the Image of God," in *Reformation Theology,* p. 299.
[27] See the excellent work by Susan Schreiner, *The Theater of His Glory: Nature and the Natural Order in the Thought of John Calvin* (The Labyrinth Press, Durham, North Carolina, 1991).
[28] Viret, *Instruction chrétienne, Tome III,* p. 529.

his admiration for this wondrous edifice which is man, created in the image and likeness of God.

> For, even though the material of which the human body is composed is no different than that used to form the bodies of wild beasts, yet, since God chose to place within it a soul of a heavenly and divine nature [for it is a spirit, as are the angels who stand in the presence of God] and of a much more excellent nature than all the other natures and creatures possessing bodies, He willed to give to this soul a dwelling place suitable to its nature and one which teaches man the excellence of his creation and the fact that he wasn't created to only fix his gaze on the earth like the beasts but to raise his eyes to heaven and consider within it the greatest works of God his Creator, as well as all within the rest of this earthly masterpiece.

Then, raising his aim to heaven itself, Philip exclaims:

> For, properly speaking, man isn't this body that we see, but the soul and spirit that we can't see, of which the body is no more than the residence, as the philosophers themselves, and particularly Plato, truly understood. And this is why Paul also calls it an "earthen vessel" which, however, God has filled with marvelous treasures (2 Cor. 4:7).[29]

You see, in passing, how the platonic note is quite naturally corrected by a realist, Aristotelian toning down, for, for Viret, the body (unlike the Platonists) isn't the soul's prison, for at the resurrection on the last day the body will rejoin the soul that preceded it to heaven.

What is quite remarkable in what we've seen of Viret's thought on the natural world is that it is still possible for him—which didn't seem nearly as easy to do for his friend and colleague John Calvin—to review (with the greatest of ease) the

---

[29] Viret, *Instruction chrétienne*, Tome III, p. 530.

created and established order of nature with, properly speaking, theological considerations. With the gradual—and more and more pervasive and restrictive—acceptance of the new scientific model as an exclusively mathematical construction of the view of the world, such a passage would (for us moderns) become more and more difficult to integrate. Today, after atomistic, mathematical materialism has broken all visible coherence of the creation, this viewpoint seems to be nearly impossible to the citizens of the new univocal cosmos of this artificial new world.[30] We could, in following the advice of a confessional Reformed pastor friend of mine, draw two conclusions from this:

1) One of the reasons why John Calvin enjoyed such fame comes from the fact that his theology was more compatible with the "clear and distinct" thought of Descartes—a univocal view of an essentially mathematical world, which would become the thinking of the future—which wasn't the same with that of Pierre Viret.

2) But to this observation we must add that Pierre Viret's anthropology goes hand in hand with a way of perceiving nature (a divine creation whose moral and spiritual scope is accessible to our minds and understanding!) which is at present foreign to us, and it is our Christian duty to recover it.

Let's continue with the extensive quotes that we've drawn from Douglas Kelly's excellent study:

> Viret then expounded at large our five bodily senses. . . . For example, he showed how the tongue and the usefulness of the human languages reflect the triune God, in whom is "the Word." . . .
>
> [W]e find Viret describing and spiritually applying the nose, the face, and the members of the human body that are attributed to God. He talked

---

[30] See the characterization of this disharmony, "all coherence gone," according to the great metaphysical poet and Reformed Anglican theologian, John Donne, at the beginning of the seventeenth century.

about the brain and our interior sensations and within that section offered interesting insights on common sense, memory, imagination, and how the Evil One disturbs us inwardly.[31]

In his conclusion Douglas Kelly then draws some reflections from the detailed examination he conducted on the complete man, the image of God, which fills a large part of the third volume of Viret's *Instruction chrétienne:*

> As an assessment, I would deem that his long and far-ranging survey of man's bodily and mental life is, so far as I can tell, correct, and though not allegorical (i.e., it accepts the full reality of both the physical aspects of the body and the events of the text of Scripture without evacuating the significance of either one of them), it is certainly more "creative" than most of the Calvinist wing of the Reformation. Perhaps we could think of Viret's long disquisition on the image of God in man as a sort of massive meditation on David's marvel over human nature in Psalm 139.[32]

Let's complete Douglas Kelly's remarkable appreciation of the third book of *Instruction chrétienne* by quoting some verses from this psalm:

> For thou hast possessed my reins: thou hast covered me in my mother's womb. I will praise thee; for I am fearfully and wonderfully made: marvellous are thy works; and that my soul knoweth right well. My substance was not hid from thee, when I was made in secret, and curiously wrought in the lowest parts of the earth. Thine eyes did see my substance, yet being unperfect; and in thy book all my members were written, which in continuance were fashioned, when as yet there was none of them. How precious also are thy thoughts unto me, O God! how great is the sum

---

[31] Kelly, "Creation, Mankind, and the Image of God," pp. 299-300.
[32] Kelly, "Creation, Mankind, and the Image of God," p. 300.

of them! If I should count them, they are more in number than the sand: when I awake, I am still with thee.

Psalm 139:13-18

Conclusion

We'll let Viret himself draw us to our conclusion. The conversation—as always in this third volume—is between Nathaniel and Philip. It's Nathaniel, the disciple, who speaks first:

> NATHANIEL: I find very shocking the folly and absurdity of those who take such pains to measure heaven and earth and to scurry here and there throughout the entire world in an attempt to understand the things contained in it and their nature, and yet at the same time they—who are no more than a handful of dust—don't know or understand how to measure themselves.
>
> For I consider it quite obvious that there is no astronomy, geometry, geography, cosmography, or any other mathematical science as necessary for man as that by which he can learn to truly understand himself and to properly measure himself according to the capacity of his own nature, in order that he might know how best to content himself within the limits of it.[33]
>
> And, concerning the mathematicians and physicians and natural philosophers [those who study the sciences] and doctors who strive after the knowledge of nature and natural things and who yet at the same time forget God and themselves instead of learning to recognize both the one and the other through the science and knowledge that God has given them of His works, I say that they are no longer worthy to be taken for physicians, natural philosophers, doctors, or mathematicians, but instead

---

[33] As Francois Rabelais—later repeated by Blaise Pascal—said, "Science without conscience is the ruin of the soul."

are only thoughtless and foolish beasts.

The teacher responds to Nathaniel:

> PHILIP: It seems to me that such people are like a man who always remained within his house to look at and handle his possessions and tools, and yet who never used them for the work they were created for, and in the meantime he forgot himself, his wife, and his children.
>
> And, concerning the physicians, if they aren't diligent in knowing their own soul and its nature and all its parts in order to be able to give it the nourishment and medicine necessary for it in order to live well and happily, and who never do anything besides study bodies and nature in order to heal others, they truly deserve to be told, "Physician, heal thyself" (Luke 4:23). For, if a doctor should truly be mocked who busies himself with healing others and doesn't know how—or doesn't care—to heal himself, a person is truly worthy of the greatest mockery who has more care not only for his own body but also for the bodies of others than he does for his own soul and his immortal nature, which is what distinguishes him from the wild beasts.

He then concludes (and we with him):

> PHILIP: Therefore it is truly necessary for all those who study natural philosophy [the sciences] to profit so well from the study of them that they can convert this knowledge into true natural theology, by which they can learn to recognize God their Creator in the nature He has created in order to reveal and make Himself known to all within it.

And Nathaniel heartily agrees:

> NATHANIEL: This is the natural philosophy and

theology that I most desire. And therefore let's return to the creation of man, of which we still have so much left to discuss.[34]

We can clearly see within this delightful conversation the full implementation of the title of this marvelous work:

> *Christian Instruction in the Doctrine of the Law and the Gospel in true Christian philosophy and theology, both natural and supernatural, and in the contemplation of the temple and the images and works of the providence of God through the entire universe; and in the history of the creation and fall and restoration of mankind*

---

[34] Viret, *Instruction chrétienne, Tome III*, pp. 423-424.

CHAPTER SIX

Pierre Viret and Natural Law

The origin of the reflections that I wish to expound on the subject of *Pierre Viret and Natural Law* occurred during a small exchange incited by a question that one of my correspondents posed to me in the autumn of 2017 concerning the role of natural law in Pierre Viret's thought. Here is the note:

> I'm currently reading through Viret's commentary on the seventh commandment and would be very grateful for your assistance with a particular matter. During his discussion of the various degrees of consanguinity, Viret discusses the importance and use of natural law. Does Viret understand by natural law the Law of God which was originally written on the hearts of men and which has since become corrupted due to man's fall? Or does he understand of it a humanistic law derived from the natural order of creation?
>
> The discussions concerning the definition and authority of natural law are rather fierce today, and I do wish to properly understand Viret's meaning. I would be most appreciative for any insight you could supply me.

Introduction

By way of introduction, we'll quote a text taken from Pierre Viret's *Métamorphose chrétienne*. Theophrastus here discusses with Jerome the revelation of God within creation and, above all, in the image of God within man:

THE IMAGE OF GOD IN MAN

THEOPHRASTUS: No one can contradict your reasons. But if we find the image of God painted so vividly in the least creature that He created, consider what image of God we'll find in man, whom God personally created and formed after His own image and likeness (Gen. 1, 2), which we can easily recognize if we diligently desire to notice it. And the conclusion of the matter we're dealing with will greatly assist us in this.

THE HIGHEST AND MOST NECESSARY KNOWLEDGE FOR MAN

And therefore let's proceed to the consideration of man from the point we stopped at in our discussion; and by it (if we aren't too slow of understanding) we'll learn the highest, the most exquisite, and the most necessary knowledge that man could ever learn, which is to know God and His providence and goodness and to known ourselves and what we must be both toward God as well as toward our neighbor. Thus, to begin this matter and to better attain the knowledge of ourselves, let's begin by the frailty and misery of man.

JEROME: I agree with you, Theophrastus, that we should begin where you say. But I'd like you to first hear a little discourse which Mercurius Trismegistus gave concerning the providence of God in the creation and formation of man. For this discourse is pretty well suited to the argument at hand, particularly concerning the providence of God. He spoke thus:

And if thou wilt see and behold this Workman, even by mortal things that are upon earth, and in the deep, consider, O Son, how Man is made and framed in the Womb; and examine diligently the skill and cunning of the Workman, and learn who it was that wrought and fashioned the beautiful and Divine shape of *Man;* who circumscribed and marked out his eyes? who bored his nostrils and ears? who opened his mouth? who stretched out and tied together his sinews? who channeled the veins? who hardened and made strong the bones? who clothed the flesh with skin? who divided the fingers and joints? who flattened and made broad the soles of the feet? who dug the pores? who stretched out the spleen? who made the Heart like a *Pyramid?* who made the Liver broad? who made the Lungs spongy, and full of holes? who made the belly large and capacious? who set to outward view the more honorable parts, and hid the shameful ones?

See how many arts in one Matter, and how many Works in one Superscription, and all exceedingly beautiful and all done in measure, and yet all differing.

Who hath made all these things? What Mother? What Father? Save only God that is not visible; that made all things by his own will.

And no man says that a statue or an image is made without a Carver or a Painter, and was this Workmanship made without a Workman? O Great Blindness! O Great Impiety! O Great Ignorance!

Never, *O Son Tat,* canst thou deprive the Workmanship of the Workman; rather, it is the best Name of all the Names of God, to call him the *Father* of all, for so he is alone; and this is his work to be the Father.[1]

I truly wanted to quote this passage from Trismegistus because it seems quite astonishing for a man who had no true knowledge of the Word of God.

THEOPHRASTUS: If those who today make an occupation and a profession of atheism, even though they desire to be considered Christians, would

---

[1] *The Divine Pymander of Hermes Mercurius Trismegistus, translated from the Arabic by John Everard [1650]* (George Redway, London, 1884), pp. 33-34. Archaic spelling and terminology has been modernized.

consider these things as closely as this poor pagan Trismegistus, despite what he was, they truly wouldn't be as brutish as they are, nor so monstrously horrible by nature.[2]

What we see in the *Métamorphose chrétienne* and *Le monde a l'empire* (a work from which this astonishing quote from the pagan Mercurius Trismegistus in praise of a God who makes Himself known through His creatures is taken) is the image of a Pierre Viret profoundly attached to the order of creation as well as to that of the Bible, orders which correspond to each other, for both have as their Author the same God, Revealer, Creator, Ordainer, Sustainer, and Providence. But Viret, a theologian with an insatiable curiosity, leans equally on the "historic" and "cultural" realities of the then past, but also—and above all—on those of his own time, a "sociological" or "literary" attention that we'll deal with here. As every attentive reader of his *Commentary on the Ten Commandments* can easily notice, he goes even further—and much further—in his interest in law and justice.

But the view that Viret had of law and justice—which I hope to address briefly in this chapter—isn't that of an exhaustive and meticulous modern legislator animated by a "positive" legal "rational" voluntarism, that of a frenzied man who furiously attempts to legislate everything. Even more, our modern lawyer or legislator—completely contrary to Pierre Viret and all Christian tradition to which he was joined—is animated by an inflexible zeal to eliminate the least trace of transcendence in the rule of law. For the intrinsic essence of God is, among many other attributes, animated by a perfect justice. It is this transcendent justice which the modern voluntarist and positive law must not allow to show through. But we must immediately add that this divine justice, in its earthly manifestation both in law as well as in morality, doesn't consist—as is the case with certain modern contemporary applications of the realities of the commandments of the Law revealed by God—simply in the judicial alignment of

---

[2] Pierre Viret, *Métamorphose chrétienne, faite par dialogues*, pp. 4-6.

elements deemed appropriate drawn from the Bible, one after another, like soldiers on parade! This is not the right method to a proper reading either of the Bible or of biblical Law!

For the Bible isn't some type of theological, ethical, and logical machine, both binary and univocal! Scripture, while affirming the absolute and infallible character of its teaching, also takes into account the realities of time and space, revealing itself throughout the course of its revelation in history as divine wisdom, a legal wisdom which fits within providential circumstances, to ordain the history of a fallen world. Thus, the Ten Commandments—the summary of the normative teaching of the Bible—must, in their moral and judicial application to the various times and places of the history of men, be read:

First, in their original sense as a divine norm of all that is just and right;

Second, as the expression of the righteous character of the divine Lawgiver;

Third, as that which must be applied through the prism of the judicial laws—*casuistic*, we would say—the appropriate biblically judicial "cases" contained in the Torah;[3]

Fourth, in order to understand them, we must take into account their interpretation by the prophets and apostles;

Fifth, they must be applied to the particular circumstances of each case with the wisdom to which the wisdom literature of the Bible testifies;

Sixth, above all, they must be read in the light of the Logos-Nomos Himself, revealed in the Gospels by the direct teaching of our divine Lawgiver, the Lord and Savior Jesus Christ;

Finally, these commandments of God must be applied in an appropriate and wise way to the specific legal circumstances

---

[3] See the exceptional pioneering article of Stephen A. Kaufman, "The Structure of Deuteronomic Law," *Maarav*, 1/2, 1978-1979 (reproduced by Western Academic Press, Santa Monica, 1979, 54 pages); Walter C. Kaiser, "The Law of Deuteronomy" *Toward Old Testament Ethics* (Zondervan, Grand Rapids, 1983), pp. 127-137; John H. Walton, "Deuteronomy: An Exposition of the Spirit of the Law," *Grace Theological Journal*, 8.2, 1987, pp. 213-225.

of various times and places within the nations of this world as they seek to be applied according to the justice and equity of nations.

The type of rigidity apparent in the inflexibly logical thought advocated by some modern commentators of the Bible (and more particularly of the Law of God) scarcely does justice to the richness and complexity of these inerrant and inspired Scriptures or of the Torah which comprises the first part of them. We must remember that the Bible also teaches us that in Jesus Christ mercy and truth have kissed as well as righteousness (or justice) and peace (Psa. 85:10)! It is within such a perspective that we must now turn to our theme, *Pierre Viret and Natural Law*.

The best way to enter into this subject is to attentively examine the text of Viret to which my correspondent referred:

> DANIEL: Though we might say that the Law of Moses was abolished with regard to the ceremonies and that it no longer obliges us concerning civil and political laws except in the ways that we have shown when we spoke of this matter, yet we must here consider what natural law requires of us. And we will find that the laws given by Moses on this matter aren't only civil and political but also natural, founded in the decency which is required in nature, as appears by the fact that even the pagans who didn't receive these laws that God gave to Moses [concerning the prohibition against marriages of near kin] nevertheless judged by the natural law written on their heart that such unions as these were neither decent nor lawful. Therefore they also issued such laws. And those who had no regard for such decency (like the Canaanites) were severely condemned and punished by God, just as Moses himself testifies (Lev. 18:24-28).[4]

---

[4] Pierre Viret, *Instruction chrétienne en la Loi et l'Évangile*, Vol. II (Édition Arthur-Louis Hofer, L'Age d'Homme, Lausanne, 2009), pp. 455-457.

First, Viret affirms a triple distinction (which has become classic both to Thomists and Calvinists) within the Law of Moses itself (the *Torah*) between:

1. The unchanging and eternal *moral law*, the Ten Commandments, and the laws of the Pentateuch which are "abolished;"
2. The *ceremonial law*, entirely accomplished in Jesus Christ, and thus null and void;
3. Certain aspects of the Torah called *judicial* and *civil laws* which, though not abolished, yet do not possess the obligatory binding force for Christian states that they possessed for Israel.

Viret's position closely follows that developed by Thomas Aquinas in his *Treatise on the Ancient Law*, a position recovered much later by John Calvin and Pierre Viret himself. For, for Thomas and his Reformed emulators, since the coming of the New Covenant in the blood of Jesus Christ, the judicial laws of the Torah no longer possess an automatic binding force—as was the case for the biblical nation of Israel. For, the coming of the Messiah, which was the spiritual (messianic) and physical (political) fulfillment of the Old Covenant, put an end once and for all to the specific judicial status of the nation of Israel as the people of God. However, the application of these judicial laws has not been utterly abrogated as was the case with the ceremonial laws. They must all be examined, and what they contain of general equity must be retained. Thus, as an expression of the equity revealed as a binding standard to Israel before the coming of the Messiah, these judicial laws preserved an exemplary practical standard of equity for all nations. Thus, as Thomas Aquinas said, they possess a legal value as models of justice, leading to the application of their concrete principles to specific judicial situations in all places and times. It is within this perspective that Viret referred the biblical civil laws concerning the lawful degrees of consanguinity to the judgment of natural law.

We may well ask: "What then does natural law here require of us?" I'll quote our text anew to better capture the meaning of Viret's very words. I've highlighted the most important:

> ... we must here consider what natural law requires of us. *And we will find that the laws given by Moses on this matter aren't only civil and political but also natural, founded in the decency which is required in nature,* as appears by the fact that even the pagans who didn't receive these laws that God gave to Moses nevertheless judged by the natural law written on their heart that such [consanguineous] unions as these were neither decent nor lawful.

Thus, according to Viret, a unity exists between the civil laws contained in the Torah, the moral law (the Ten Commandments), and natural law as it is expressed in the legislation of pagan yet "civil" or "decent" nations. If pagans who didn't receive their civil laws directly from God (as was the case for ancient Israel) still followed this Law, then what is just within the laws decreed by these pagans comes from the fact that by *nature* (that is, by the stable moral order of creation recognized by the honest conscience of every individual) these laws are printed on the heart of men created in the image of God. The fact that these laws decreed by pagans present a greater or lesser conformity to the moral law (that is, to the Decalogue and to its concrete application through the civil laws of the Torah) is the result of their greater or lesser distance from God.

Thus we must recognize that these pagans—even though they remain pagan—were clearly often more capable of understanding and following the civil standards contained in the Law of God (the Torah) than are the post-Christian apostates of our day. This is exactly what Viret already stated, with a certain amount of rancor, in concluding his remarkable quote from Mercurius Trismegistus with Theophrastus' very strong language addressed to the pseudo-Reformed people of his time—and of ours!

THEOPHRASTUS: If those who today make an occupation and a profession of atheism, even though they desire to be considered Christians, considered these things as closely as this poor pagan Trismegistus, despite what he was, they truly wouldn't be as savage as they are, *nor so monstrously horrible by nature.*[5]

What would he think of these pseudo-Christian people of our day who are *so monstrously horrible by nature* that they are unable to distinguish the human character of a baby in its mother's womb, the Church that Pierre Viret, even in his time, desired to see "raised up" or *disciplined?*

The conformity of the essential contents of the legislation of various ancient pagans to the "law of nature" such as it is expressed in the civil laws revealed in the Torah can do nothing but surprise us. The closeness of meaning between these pagan laws and the ethical and judicial principles of the Decalogue clearly proves the fact that both positive revealed law and natural law are expressions, distinct but necessarily similar, of the eternal law, the immutable reflection of the righteous character of God. This agreement between natural law and the Ten Commandments was often affirmed by the Reformers. Here are a few examples taken from the remarkable book by Stephen J. Casselli, *Divine Rule Maintained: Anthony Burgess, Covenant Theology, and the Place of the Law in Reformed Scholasticism:*

> Luther, for example, argued that "natural law is clearly and exactly summarized on Mt. Sinai."[6]

John Calvin in his introduction to his *Exposition of the Ten Commandments* wrote:

> Now that inward law, which we have above described as written, even engraved, upon the hearts of all, in

---
[5] Pierre Viret, *Métamorphose chrétienne*, p. 6.
[6] Stephen J. Casselli, *Divine Rule Maintained: Anthony Burgess, Covenant Theology, and the Place of the Law in Reformed Scholasticism* (Reformation Heritage Books, Grand Rapids, MI, 2016), p. 48.

a sense asserts the very same things that are to be learned from the two Tables.[7]

Calvin also wrote:

> Now, . . . it is evident that the law of God which we call moral, is nothing else than the testimony of the natural law, and of that conscience which God has engraven on the minds of men."[8]

This position was also shared by Theodore Beza, Peter Vermigli, Girolamo Zanchi, Franciscus Junius, William Perkins, and many other Reformed theologians of the sixteenth and seventeenth centuries.

Viret therefore affirms that the judicial laws of the Torah (formulated by Moses under divine inspiration) which deal with these questions concerning the prohibition of marriage within certain degrees of consanguinity are not merely judicial and civil (concerning law and policy), but possess the *natural* character of that "decency"—that sense of what is decent, just, and right—required by nature.

But how then does Viret define what is *natural*? Is it by the abstract reasoning (an indirect result of the mathematicization of the sciences) of modern natural law theories, or in some other way? He instead defines the forbidden degrees of consanguinity in a (properly speaking) legal and sociological manner by quoting from the legislation of a number of pagan nations which, having no direct knowledge of the Mosaic laws on this subject, nevertheless judged (in a largely unanimous way), through the witness of the natural law written on the hearts of these numerous legislators, that such consanguineous unions were neither "decent," "just," nor "legally admissible." This is the reason why many pagan nations formulated just laws forbidding such consanguineous marital unions which were largely in conformity with the judicial legislation that we find in the Bible.

---

[7] Casselli, *Divine Rule Maintained*, p. 48.
[8] Casselli, *Divine Rule Maintained*, p. 48, n. 18.

> For when the Gentiles, which have not the law [the revealed law, the Torah], do by nature [by the workings of *natural law*] the things contained in the law [of Moses], these, having not the law [revealed and written in the Bible], are a law unto themselves [by the true testimony of their conscience]: which shew the work of the law written in their hearts, their conscience also bearing witness, and their thoughts the mean while accusing or else excusing one another [in full conformity to the law of Moses].
>
> Romans 2:14-15

Viret concludes with a negative argument from the fact that such "indecent" consanguineous unions were permitted by the Canaanites. Thus God's condemnation of these nations (as described by Moses in Leviticus 18:24-28) constitutes additional proof of the just nature of this natural law as it was followed by the legislation of pagans who were less morally corrupt than the Canaanites.

It's important to note here that Pierre Viret, in good biblical Aristotelian thinking, didn't limit the testimony of natural law to the internal conscience of man, in fact difficult to discern objectively.[9] But he instead uncovered it within the objective testimonies found in the legislation of pagan nations whose laws on many points were often largely in agreement with those of the civil laws of the Torah. Yet we notice a tendency among the Puritans in the middle of the seventeenth century to narrow the application of natural law to the sole domain of man's internal conscience by paying very little attention to the civil legislation of other nations, pagan or otherwise. This last—as well as many other aspects of seventeenth century culture—was then more and more handed over to the ideological, philosophical, and scientific currents dominating the era, tendencies always

---

[9] For Viret it didn't seem reasonable to affirm (as a great number of Church fathers did) that this conformity of laws within many pagan nations to the standards of the Torah on such questions provided a direct influence on the Hebraic Law or on the knowledge that they had of revelations even more ancient than that given by God to the patriarchs.

increasingly hostile to the public nature of the demands of the Law of God. But, as Stephen Casselli testifies, this wasn't yet the case even in the second part of the sixteenth century:

> The comments of the bishop of Winchester, William Day (1529-1596), on Romans 2:14-15 are typical. He explained that when Paul speaks of the Gentiles keeping the law he does not mean that they keep it fully out of a knowledge of the truth, but "because they did many things, which the Law *prescribed,* for in *making* publick Laws, and in *giving* private precepts, they did *prescribe,* and *give in precepts, honest* things, and forbid things *dishonest* [by natural law], even as *the Law of Moses* itself did.[10]

In passing (and to conclude this section), I will be so bold as to make a few personal remarks:

1. Both the legal and comparative method used here is surprisingly similar to that of Aristotle who on many ethical points arrives at similar conclusions to those of Pierre Viret.
2. This also explains why, when I worked as a porter at the Lausanne station throughout the 1970's, many Africans, during conversations I had with them, expressed their horror at the very idea that parents would murder their own offspring through abortion. They came, quite simply, from pagan nations less corrupt than our Pays de Vaud, a post-Christian, antinomian, and apostate Swiss canton. These pagan African nations still considered the arrival of a child as a divine blessing and thus as a full human being worthy of protection by law.
3. Finally, in this perspective we can understand much better the true scope, in relation to the *natural law* of the pagans, of the following text from Deuteronomy:

> Behold, I have taught you statutes and judgments, even as the LORD my God commanded me, that ye

---
[10] Casselli, *Divine Rule Maintained,* p. 50.

> should do so in the land whither ye go to possess it. Keep therefore and do them; for this is your wisdom and your understanding in the sight of the nations, which shall hear all these statutes, and say, Surely this great nation is a wise and understanding people. For what nation is there so great, who hath God so nigh unto them, as the LORD our God is in all things that we call upon him for? And what nation is there so great, that hath statutes and judgments so righteous as all this law, which I set before you this day?
>
> Deuteronomy 4:5-8

This remainder of a natural knowledge of good and evil is what makes possible the pagans' admiration for the divinely inspired laws of the people of God which this text of Deuteronomy describes. The conscience and righteous legislation of these pagan peoples reveal the existence of a true *natural law,* from which their conscience and sense of justice were not yet cauterized, as they are so largely for us today in the West.[11] This conscience, still animated by a certain amount of justice, objectively testified to the pagans' true knowledge of the *law of nature,* as was no longer the case with the Canaanites, the ancient world before the flood, the cities of the plain (Sodom and Gomorrah), and with our post-Christian world. The conscious rejection of natural law and then of divine law has cauterized the conscience of our legislators, lawyers, and ecclesiastics, always leading them more and more to call evil good and good evil.

The ancients, as pagan as they were, yet possessed a certain amount of honesty of conscience and thus, according to Pierre Viret (following the entire Bible), they could still appreciate the wisdom and understanding of Hebrew legislation! But (to give an approximate date) since the exclusion of all connection between public law and the revealed Law of God (the Torah) by the famous Dutch jurist Hugo Grotius (1583-1645), and above all with the growing influence of a rationalist, purely subjective

---

[11] We would call it *secularized,* a word which means *without God.*

natural law[12] such as Samuel von Pufendorf (1632-1694) and his school embraced, our legislation in the West has progressively shown itself to be less and less capable of legislating—or judging, of *speaking justice*—according to the general objective good and according to justice! This is the civil reality which the psalmist was already well aware of:

> Shall the throne of iniquity have fellowship with thee, which frameth mischief by a law? They gather themselves together against the soul of the righteous, and condemn the innocent blood. But the LORD is my defence; and my God is the rock of my refuge. And he shall bring upon them their own iniquity, and shall cut them off in their own wickedness; yea, the LORD our God shall cut them off.
>
> Psalm 94:20-23

Viret's argument "from a *natural law*" derives all its force from the fact that a true similarity exists between a specific just pagan legislation on these questions of illicit matrimonial unions and the civil (or political) laws of the Mosaic Law. What Viret seeks to communicate to us is that this is visible not by the knowledge of some "theory of natural law" but by the pagan legislative models largely in conformity to the Mosaic civil law. They were established from examples of specific legislation of pagans animated by "decent and just" principles on these questions of sexual ethic. These moral and civil principles contrasted fully with those of various ungodly nations and, in particular, with the Canaanites. These last had reached the height of their sexual iniquity, having without doubt even attempted to judicially legitimize such consanguineous unions which, by all lawful honesty, were perfectly inadmissible. Thus, for Viret, the law of nature (or natural law) was never that abstract notion that it became with Samuel von Pufendorf in the seventeenth and eighteenth centuries—under the influence of both the voluntarist

---

[12] Though while still maintaining for a time a certain sense of objective natural law.

and subjective philosophical rationalism as well as the model of experimental mathematicization adulated by the new Newtonian sciences. For Viret, *natural law* consisted of the attentive and accumulated observation of the laws of decent pagans dealing with these matters. In this he followed the method elaborated by Aristotle and afterwards developed by Thomas Aquinas, who sought to establish a *law of nature* not from purely abstract reasoning (as is almost always the case today for the modern theoreticians of natural law) but by the careful study of the legal practice of various pagan nations still animated by a "decent" spirit.

Just like the biblical textual critics attached to the classic Reformed tradition of the *ecclesiastical* or *received* text separate the trustworthy manuscripts—discovered according to the Greek or Hebrew texts of the Bible revealing a near *unanimity*—from those which are openly defective, so in the same way the jurists of ancient natural law separated the documents proceeding from "decadent, unwholesome, indecent" sources, and only retained as models of a true natural law those which came from a "healthy and decent" civil tradition. Having the advantage over Aristotle of possessing within the moral and civil biblical law a reliable touchstone, the Christian jurist scholastics could easily distinguish between "decent" and "indecent" legislation. This remarkable work of discernment was carried out in the thirteenth century under a very well-informed hand by Thomas Aquinas in his *Treatise on the Ancient Law* (the Mosaic Law) and later in the sixteenth century by Pierre Viret in his *Simple Exposition of the Ten Commandments of the Law in the Form of a Conversation*.[13] Today scholars—even Christian ones—scarcely know how to distinguish their left hand from their right!

For Pierre Viret the historical character of this natural

---

[13] Pierre Viret, *Exposition familière sur les Dix Commandements de la Loi faite en forme de Dialogue* (Jean Gerard, Geneva, 1564). This work has been translated into English and published in ten volumes under the titles: Pierre Viret, *No Other God; Nothing Like God; Taking His Name in Vain; Remember the Sabbath Day; Honor Thy Father and Mother; Thou Shalt Not Kill; Thou Shalt Not Commit Adultery; Thou Shalt Not Steal; Defend the Truth;* and *Thou Shalt Not Covet.*

law assumed a great importance, for this represented an objective confirmation—both *natural* and *historical*—of the laws of the Torah, a justification drawn from the legal practice of pagan nations legislating on these matters of consanguinity. This shows us that Pierre Viret clearly founded his conception of natural law (or natural justice)—what he prefers to call *the law of nature*—on principles utterly foreign to those practiced by the majority of the most recent scholars who espouse a very *modern* conception of natural law. These "decent" civil practices discovered in the civil custom of pagan nations by the concrete testimony—in referring to this single example—of national legislation on this question of consanguineous sexual unions were, for former Christian theology, a corroboration of the force and the judicial veracity of the biblical laws of the Torah.

This *theonomic* interpretation is fully confirmed by a passage taken from the first volume of Viret's *Instruction chrétienne*. Let's hear the text:

> DANIEL: But it's another matter with His eternal revealed will [a reference to what Thomas Aquinas calls the *eternal law*] and with the matters that He has once declared that He considers to be good or evil forever [written by Him in the Torah], and which concern their substance [their *essence*, opposed to their *accidents* or that which is nonessential], and which aren't only like accessories [accidentals], as are the ceremonies; for in this way He has never changed and never issued a Law by which He approved of idolatry, blasphemy, adultery, murder, and other such wickedness which He once for all condemned in His Law, which is nothing more than a testimony of His eternal will [the *eternal* divine law, a scholastic expression] and of that natural law [law of nature, creational law] which is naturally [by the act of creation] imprinted on the heart of men, by which He has placed within them a stamp of His eternal will which has never been effaced.[14]

---

[14] Viret, *Instruction Chrétienne*, Tome I (Édition Arthur-Louis Hofer), p. 458.

CHAPTER SEVEN

Natural Law Applied: the Diversity of Laws and the Modern Abuse of Natural Law

A few pages prior to the quote ending the last chapter, in a section entitled "The diversity of civil laws according to the diversities of people and countries," Pierre Viret explains the characteristics suitable to the judicial liberty which various national legislations witness to on certain aspects of law:

> TIMOTHY: But couldn't God have given various ways of living to men according to the capacity of each people group and every nation? For we see from experience that laws and customs exist in one country which are very suitable to it, but which don't exist in another country and wouldn't be suitable to it, either. For how great a diversity of laws, customs, and manners of life do we see among men, particularly in the matter of law and politics, which seem to be utterly contrary to each other? Yet they don't cease to be just and equitable in their place, and quite suitable for those to whom they are given. Thus it follows that if a law was good and just in one country but wasn't in another, that the fault doesn't proceed from the law but from the diversity which exists among men and among circumstances, times, places, and peoples.[1]

Thus we see that natural and divine (eternal and revealed) law which is always just in its substance mustn't be called into question here, but instead the fault lies in what

---
[1] Viret, *Instruction chrétienne*, Tome I, p. 455.

we could call the diversities created by the "collective sins" of certain wicked customs belonging to one nation or another, as well as the necessities of time and space. For example, the law could in one nation forbid theft and could also authorize theft by the Welfare State, both of the rich as well as to the detriment of the poor, all while cracking down on various thefts judged worthy of condemnation. The infraction of the law "Thou shalt not steal" by particular laws decreed by this nation would in no way weaken the general scope of the commandment forbidding and judicially penalizing theft just as its specific civil (casuistic) determinations.

Timothy then applies this principle to the diversity of laws in relation to the diversity of nations themselves, but also applies it to the civil and ceremonial laws of the people of God, both as they concern the Old as well as the New Covenant.

> TIMOTHY: And, without setting forth human legal systems (which are very different from each other), let's turn simply to the Law of God and consider whether we find it the same in all respects. How many times did God command something to the Jews which He didn't choose to subject not only other peoples to who preceded the coming of our Lord Jesus Christ but ourselves also who have received the Word of God through their ministry? For how many things did He abolish by the New Covenant which were strictly commanded and observed in the Old Covenant and which couldn't then be omitted without greatly offending God and without grievous punishment against those to whom they had been commanded?[2]

To this fundamental question of the current validity (or non-validity) of certain laws of the Old Testament for the nations of Christendom, in a section entitled "The reasons for the diversity of civil laws and the difference which exists between the laws given in physical matters and those which pertain to

---
[2] Viret, *Instruction chrétienne*, Tome I, pp. 455-456.

spiritual things," Viret sets forth a difference which recalls the illuminating distinction advanced by Dietrich Bonhoeffer who here recaptured (and corrected) a thought of Martin Luther's, not that between two kingdoms of similar value, but between the realities that he calls *ultimate* and *penultimate*.[3]

Concerning the *ultimate*, no difference exists in Jesus Christ between male and female, master and servant, officer and enlisted man; concerning the *penultimate*, this hierarchical order is upheld even by Christians—indeed, it's even reinforced by its foundation in God Himself: we must obey the magistrate for the sake of conscience, for God Himself appoints all exercise of lawful authority on earth. For, with this *penultimate* order, we're dealing with our life here below, that which concerns the order of creation (nature) and the commandments of God. For this order is always valid in this earthy life, and it will experience not an abolition but a transfiguration in the *ultimate* world to come. Even more, it is by obedience to the criteria, references, and standards of the *penultimate* order that our *ultimate* life in Christ is constructed. Obedience in the little things precedes and establishes the obedience we owe to the greatest things! It is by honoring her husband and by correctly raising her children that a Christian wife becomes more and more spiritual; likewise, by conducting himself as a good husband and father, a Christian man continues the work of sanctification. Let's here consider a very modern example.

A contemporary Reformed American theologian, David M. VanDrunen, also attempted to salvage Martin Luther's theory of the two kingdoms for a natural law without any strict connection to the Decalogue.[4] But we must clearly distinguish between

---

[3] For this aspect of Dietrich Bonhoeffer's thought, see the fourth chapter, "Ultimate and Penultimate Realities," of his *Ethics* (Macmillan, New York, 1965). See also Georg Huntemann's work, *The Other Bonhoeffer: an Evangelical Reassessment of Dietrich Bonhoeffer* (Baker Books, Grand Rapids, MI, 1993).

[4] There exists today in the American Reformed midst a renewed interest in natural law. See Stephen J. Grahill, *Rediscovering the Natural Law in Reformed Theological Ethics* (Eerdmans, Grand Rapids, 2006). A controversial figure in this renewal is the prolific author, David VanDrunen, *Law and Bible* (S.P.C.K., London, 2013); *Living in God's Two Kingdoms: a Biblical Vision for Christianity and Culture* (Crossway Books, 2010);

his position and that defended by Dietrich Bonhoeffer, both seeking to recover (though in very different ways) the thought of the great German Reformer.

For Luther, theology must be founded solely on a realist, precise, and grammatically exact doctrinal reading of the Bible—that is, of the Gospel. In this way he sought to restore the authority of the dogmas, the theological universals revealed by God Himself. Ethics, on the contrary, represented for him an inferior domain, abandoned (to a certain degree) to man's free choice. The Law-Word of God was thus in his eyes normative for theology but not for ethics (in rather guarded proportions, for his thought in this realm had the tendency to contradict itself). This was a breach opened by the Lutheran Reformation in favor of what we call *secularization* (that is, nominalist and antinomian atheism), which is a distinctive feature of the modern world. The practical domain was (at least partially) abandoned to the sole judgment of man's free choice.

David VanDrunen goes even further (at least in part, but certainly in an even more dangerous way) with his Two Kingdom theory. For him the Kingdom of the Church has as its standard the Law-Word of God, both in what concerns its theology as well as its ethics. On the other hand, the culture of the Kingdom of the world must not be placed under the standards of the Law-Word of God but under those of a natural law independent of biblical standards and submitted to a consensual natural law which scarcely has any affinity to the Decalogue at all. If Luther opened the door to a world independent of God and His Law, David VanDrunen attempts to reconcile the obedience of Christians to the modern world, without God or Law, by depriving this world of all connection to the obedience required by God's Law. We must remember that the "testimony of Jesus" is noth-

---

Natural Law and the Two Kingdoms: a Study in the Development of Reformed Social Thought (Eerdmans, Grand Rapids, 2010); *Divine Covenants and Moral Order: a Biblical Theology of Natural Law* (Eerdmans, Grand Rapids, 2014), etc. On the subject of the debatable theology of David VanDrunen, see the very enlightening article by John Frame, "Review of David Van Drunen's *A Biblical Case for Natural Law*," May 10, 2012: https://frame-poythress.org/review-of-david-van-drunens-a-biblical-case-for-natural-law/.

ing other than "the spirit of prophecy" (Rev. 19:10) and that, as mentioned previously, this "spirit of prophecy" is the application of the red-hot iron of the Law-Word of God to the sins of the world. This has one of two effects: either of drawing the ungodly to repentance and faith or of hardening them in their sin and unbelief.

Dietrich Bonhoeffer's position (mentioned earlier) moves in a completely different direction. For him, all earthly realities—which include the Church militant on earth—are subject to the divine Law-Word. He calls this the domain of the *penultimate* realities. By contrast, founded on the immutable foundation of this Law-Word of God and the established order of creation, the Gospel surpasses the order and scope of the Law and creation. Yet it does it without contradicting either God's Law or the order of creation, and at the renewal of all things it will achieve what will be similar to a general transfiguration of the elect people of God. This heavenly reality certainly already exists in part here below in believers as a deposit (or firstfruit) of the *ultimate* realities which are spoken of in the Beatitudes. Thus this is the domain of Bonhoeffer's *ultimate* realities.

Moreover, Christ's teaching in the Sermon on the Mount, addressed to the life of the Church but also to the world, seeks to rectify the pharisaic legalism of the Jewish leaders of His time by expounding a just understanding of the Law of God. But, we must immediately add, it is in the observance and practice of God's commandments that the foundation of the life of the Beatitudes is found. These are *ultimate* realities: to love God above all, which is a much higher standard of love than to love our neighbor as ourselves. These *ultimate* realities (to which, for example, the experience of the martyrs testify) then consist in exceeding the earthly *penultimate* realities, those of faithful obedience (through Christ and by the power of the Holy Spirit) to the commandments of God and in a submission to the order of creation. This obedience is required both for pagans as well as Christians. The final judgment will be given according to, or in consequence of, the rejection of this obedience. The obedience of Christians flows from the perfect active obedience of Christ to all God's commandments, an obedience which is imputed to the believer through faith, a free gift of God which leads him to fulfill the good works prepared for him in advance (before the foundation of the world) by God.

David VanDrunen's theology leads to what Cornelius Van Til calls "the integration into the void."[5] That of Dietrich Bonhoeffer leads to "the integration to heaven." The first leads to the increase of the perdition of the world and the reign of darkness; the second to heavenly salvation and the Kingdom of God, for by it the Church becomes the salt of the earth and the light of the world. It is only in the heavenly Jerusalem that God—and God alone—will be the light, both physical and spiritual, of men, that is, of His well-beloved.

We find a seductive intellectual operation similar to that of David VanDrunen's Two Kingdom theology in the *Personalism* of Emmanuel Mounier, an effort undertaken to disarm the Catholic Church's resistance to the modern world (in modernist liberalism, socialist consensualism, and communism) by the distinction that he invents between the *person,* who possesses a spiritual and Christian character, and the *individual,* an element of his being reserved for the material sphere—that of science, technology, economy, and politics. Only the physical material part of man (which is the *individual*) is engaged in the world of the laws of physics and in the politics of a modernity which has loosed its moorings from the standards of the Law of God and the creation order. This is, under the name of a reforming Catholicism, a return to the Kantian dualism of the phenomena and noumenon, a duality which opposes scientific realities to that of the faith in a fractured world where a double truth reigns, a universe split in half.

The very surprising rallying by certain aspects of the French Roman Catholic philosopher Jacques Maritain to this vision of the human being divided into two parts between a

---

[5] See Cornelius Van Til, *The Psychology of Religion,* as quoted in "The Psychology of Religion: Integration into the Void," in Rousas J. Rushdoony, *By What Standard* (Ross House Books, 1995), pp. 65-80.

spiritual (heavenly) *person* and a material (earthly) *individual* at the beginning of the 1930's greatly favored the success of this political-religious ideology which affirms that Christian "values" only apply to the spiritual person of man, whereas the individual can otherwise support (and even labor to encourage) the apostate culture of a world radically hostile to the Christian faith and above all to Jesus Christ.

This dualist, schizophrenic, and Gnostic system would permit the *person* to live a dedicated Christian life while the *individual* gives themselves over to a world without faith or law.[6] Later, this dualism opens the door to the practice of the *praxis* of a social collaboration between seemingly very zealous Christians and Marxists. The celebrated work of Henri de Lubac, *Surnaturel*, with those of Jacques Maritain, *Primauté de Spiritual* and *Humanisme intégral: Problèmes spirituals d'une nouvelle chrétienté*, provide a major theological and philosophical caution to a Gnostic dualism which permits Catholics who adopt it both to hedge their bets and to participate in the best of both worlds—Christian and antichristian—all while living in the heart of modern society as well as in the bosom of the Churches. By dividing human nature into a (Christian) *person* and a (worldly) *individual*, all need for Christian resistance to the (modern) world disappears. This was the major preparation of the way that led to the *aggionamento*—the adaptation to the world—of Vatican II.

Let's return now to Pierre Viret and to the question of the current validity (or non-validity) of particular civil laws of the Old Testament for the nations (what is called "Christendom").

> DANIEL: There are many reasons which offer a satisfactory answer to your question. First, it's no

---

[6] Such a spiritual-material dualism is found in the gnosis of the Cathars, for example, in which the man (or woman) who becomes fully "spiritual" can commit any amount of moral turpitude while all the while remaining "pure" in his own eyes, for his comportment concerns only his body and not his spirit. A similar dualism also exists in certain Darbyites, in which the most intense spirituality can be joined to the most depraved and most carnal life without the alleged heavenly "communion" of the believer with God being in any way affected. We can find similar tendencies in certain aspects of Puritanism.

surprise if a vast diversity exists and if a contradiction and inconsistency is often revealed in human laws. For the men who write them are fickle and inconsistent. And, because they often err either by ignorance or by being dominated by their passions, it's often necessary for their later laws to correct their earlier.

TIMOTHY: But, to the contrary, it also often happens that their later laws are worse than the first and that they abolish other laws which are better than the new ones.

DANIEL: This is much worse. But none of this can happen to God.
  Second, we mustn't judge spiritual and heavenly matters [*ultimate* realities] in the same way as physical and earthly matters [*penultimate* realities]. For we see daily by experience that there are many laws in the political realm which would be as unsuitable and harmful in some countries (if people chose to observe them) as they are suitable and beneficial in other countries. This is why God didn't will to subject other people—not even Christians—to all the civil laws that He gave to the people of Israel; but instead (concerning many laws) He left this to the liberty of all, on the condition that this liberty be always regulated by the standard of His [righteous] will and by the eternal and unchangeable Law [the *eternal* law revealed in the *natural* law and in the Decalogue, the *moral* law and its application in the *civil* law] that we're about to begin discussing.

We see here how Viret employs not only the *natural* law to determine what is just and good but also the *eternal* law, as long as in both cases the freedom of this human legislation is always ruled by "the standard of His will and by the eternal and unchangeable Law," the eternal law—the mind of God—being, for us humans, analogically refracted by all other forms of law, particularly by the positive and revealed law of the *moral* law (the immutable Decalogue) and its application in the *civil* laws (adapted to the various circumstances of time and space, though always remaining just).⁷ Let's resume our reading of Viret.

> DANIEL: For these laws which He has left to Christian freedom concern the body and possessions, the preservation of human society, and external order. In such things there will necessarily be a vast diversity because they are composed of various qualities [accidents] subject to various changes [*penultimate* realities]. Therefore it is necessary for the lawgiver to consider the capacity and the ease or difficulty of the persons he is dealing with, and the time and place in which they exist.
>
> But it's another matter with the soul and the things which pertain exclusively to it [*ultimate* realities]. For it isn't composed of as many pieces as the body is. Therefore it isn't subject to such changes and diversities [*penultimates*]; and the things which pertain to it aren't temporal but eternal [*ultimate*]. Because of this, the laws given concerning it must extend much further and must last for a much longer time [for the *ultimate* realities concern our salvation and eternal life].

We find ourselves here in the presence of the Medieval distinction—not opposition!—between matter and form, body and soul, expressed by Viret in terms which will not immediately be identified by his sixteenth century Reformed reader as bearing the mark of this scholasticism which was then so vigorously rejected, for example, in the writings of Viret's colleague and dear friend John Calvin.

In his next section Viret deals with "The affinity existing between the civil and ceremonial laws, and their true use." Timothy begins:

---

⁷ See Jean-Marc Berthoud, "Une analyse structurelle des diverses lois: éternelle, naturelle, humaine et divine," in *Le règne terrestre de Dieu* (L'Age d'Homme, Lausanne, 2011), pp. 412-433.

> TIMOTHY: But God didn't only take this way with the civil laws [the human law, the civil and criminal code], but also in the laws He gave in matters of religion which concern the soul. And, what's even more, concerning the civil laws themselves that He gave, weren't they given to assist in the observance of those matters which exclusively concern the soul?

Here he raises the question of the relationship between Church and State, between the spiritual and temporal powers, and in particular he refers to the support that a God-fearing State must render to the faithful Christian Church; then of the permanence or temporary nature of such laws.

> DANIEL: I don't deny what you say, but you must consider that this change of laws and ordinances that God employed even in religious matters only applies to the ceremonies, which are external things, and not to the substance of the immutable will of God [the *eternal* law].

Here Viret is dealing with the question of the relation between the temporal and eternal, between the external elements of the Law and civil society, their "accidents" and their "substance," their justice. We see once again that he employs a classical scholastic distinction while modifying its expression but not its content and meaning. He is speaking here of the dual distinction between form and matter and between universals and accidents. For him the word *substance*—"the actual substance of the immutable will of God"—is of capital importance. For Viret is in no way a relativist in morality or a nominalist in philosophy. As the moderate realist he always proves to be on the philosophical plane, the substance inherent in the argument (its form, here the doctrine or the universally valid law drawn from the Bible) is of dogmatic, capital, vital importance. Thus it is within the "substance" that we find the immutable teaching of God.

Viret then explains the importance of the "changeable" laws of the Torah, both ceremonial and civil:

> DANIEL: Therefore the ceremonial laws have a strong affinity with the civil. For, just as the civil laws are given for the preservation of the civil order and also to assist in leading men to render the obedience they owe to God, so also in a similar way the ceremonial laws serve to maintain ecclesiastical order and to fashion men for the true worship of God.
>
> But because the ways by which this is done can be various, and because some of them can be suitable for one time and in particular places among particular people but wouldn't be suitable for others, God has allowed much greater freedom on the condition that the rule I already mentioned previously is still observed. For these things are in this way like indifferent matters; and the change that occurs in them doesn't proceed from God or from a fickleness in His will but from our weakness and fickleness and because God in His goodness willingly chooses to condescend to our ignorance and limited ability.[8]

Here we see the Calvinist doctrine of *accommodation*, though expressed by a term generally used in Patristic and later Orthodox thought: God's *condescension*, "His condescending to our weakness." Thomas Aquinas would have used the more philosophical term *analogy*, God's revelation to men being neither univocal nor equivocal, but analogical. Neither absolutely, mathematically exact, nor irrationally inexact, but exact—in an accommodated or condescending manner—in analogical proportion to our intellectual capacity as creatures made in the image of God and the precise object under consideration.

> DANIEL: For the doctrine of the Law is a study and knowledge of God's will which is, as it were, born with man in his creation, inasmuch as God has printed it

---
[8] Viret, *Instruction chrétienne, Tome I,* pp. 456-457.

on his heart and has endowed him with this grace (as well as others which He has given to him) when He fashioned and formed him "in His image and likeness" (Gen. 1:26-27). But, because it is greatly effaced and obscured by the sin which came afterward, we must come to the knowledge and understanding of the Gospel ["the new law," in scholastic terms] which is not natural to us, as is that of the Law, nor a possession from our first creation [the second creation being our *regeneration*, the firstfruits of this ultimate *recreation* which will come directly from heaven on the last day] as this is, but is from regeneration, redemption, and restoration, which is revealed to us by the Son of God, who has carried us to "the bosom of the Father" (John 1:18).[9]

Thus for Viret the Law and the Gospel are distinct realities, the knowledge of the Law being natural (*penultimate*) while that resulting from the Gospel is supernatural (*ultimate*), which restores in us the sure and certain testimony of the Law and our ability to obey its commandments (at least in part). This understanding and this renewed will come to us through special (and not natural) intervention—here Viret doesn't use the word *supernatural*—proceeding from the incarnation and work of Christ which is applied to us for our salvation by the Holy Spirit, received from the Father by the Son and sent by Jesus Christ to His Church at Pentecost. In speaking of the continuity existing between the Law and the Gospel, Viret wrote on the subject of the Law:

> For Christ and His own never taught anything contrary to it [the Law], but to the contrary approved and fulfilled it. This is why Paul calls Jesus Christ the End, the Perfection, and the Fulfillment of the Law, and the foundation of the prophets and apostles (Rom. 10:4; Eph. 2:20). And therefore he clearly explained before Agrippa that he taught "none other things than those

---

[9] Viret, *Instruction chrétienne*, Tome I, p. 685.

which the prophets and Moses did say" (Acts 26:22).[10]

Viret continues on this theme of the harmony between the Law and the Gospel:

> Similarly, our Lord Jesus Christ often sent the Jews to Moses' testimony, saying that he had testified of Him, and He sent them to the Scriptures, just as we already said (John 5:46-47). Likewise this agreement of the Law and the prophets with Jesus Christ was revealed in His transfiguration because the apostles saw Him "with Moses and Elijah" (Matt. 17:2-4; Luke 9:29-30). And when He opened the hearts of His disciples on the road to Emmaus, He expounded to them the testimonies written of Himself in the Law, the Psalms, and the prophets (Luke 24:25-27).

On the unity between Moses, the prophets, Jesus Christ, and the apostles, Viret also wrote:

> Thus we can easily understand by this that, just as the prophets who were sent by God after Moses were like expositors of the Law and the doctrine that He set forth to His Church both through him as well as through the patriarchs who were before him, so also our Lord Jesus and His apostles were the true expositors of all the former teaching and were those by whom the final word concerning the entire doctrine of salvation was revealed and declared to the Church.[11]

In the French phrase *dernière détermination* (translated in the above quote as "final word"), we must note that the word *détermination,* as Arthur-Louis Hofer indicates, means "a decision on a controversial teaching, particularly in matters of doctrine." This notion of *détermination* was a standard concept in scholastic thought. This technical sense is also that of Pierre

---
[10] Viret, *Instruction chrétienne, Tome I*, p. 686.
[11] Viret, *Instruction chrétienne, Tome I*, p. 687.

Viret. If I may be permitted to transcribe one of my former writings, I'll show what Thomas Aquinas understood by this term:

> Thus we see that we are no longer allowed to put into practice the ceremonial precepts of the divine law, since they have been definitively accomplished by the perfect work of Christ. For He shed His own blood, once for all, in order to fulfill all these figures. Yet this isn't the same [according to Thomas] with the laws which concern the precepts called *civil,* for the moral principles (the second table of the Decalogue) command specific applications (the civil laws) which we must not pass by. Thus the civil law, with its *déterminations,* gives us a topographical description of the civil terrain which the specific moral principles of the Decalogue cover. These principles are expressed by the Ten Commandments which themselves have a general universal character. This universal character of the moral commandment must be applied to the specific circumstances in which we live. This application of *moral* principles (exclusive to the second table of the Decalogue) to particular circumstances is the expression of the civil law. This wholesome civil casuistry that the Torah (and the entire Bible) contains is what Thomas Aquinas calls the *détermination.*[12]

After agreeing with Timothy that man experiences the need to justify the laws he formulates by an authority above himself and superior to himself—whether true (God) or imaginary (an idol)—Daniel continues:

> DANIEL: Furthermore, though darkness has fallen on the human mind because of sin, yet a stamp of the knowledge of God remains on men's hearts which constrains all to acknowledge that there is a sovereign and divine Power to which all men must necessarily

---

[12] Jean-Marc Berthoud, "Thomas Aquinas and Politics," originally published in Jean-Marc Berthoud, *Le règne terrestre de Dieu,* pp. 434-504.

be subject, whether they will or no, and that this sovereign power is the eternal God. Therefore no person exists, no matter how wretched he might be (if he isn't entirely more beastly than the brute beasts) who isn't in some way moved when the authority of God is set forth and who doesn't fear punishment when someone tells him that God has commanded or forbidden what he intends to do if he says or does the contrary, particularly when we have a high opinion of those who speak to us and when we consider them honest men.[13]

Consequently we are forced to note to how great a degree modernity has withdrawn itself from this universal consciousness of God which still largely existed in Pierre Viret's day. It would be very rare to find anyone today who would react like the common people of his time. The skeptical spirit of the former Pyrrhonism of Sextus Empiricus (a philosopher active in AD 190) and that of Michel de Montaigne (1533-1592) expressed with such eloquence in his famous *Essays* is, to our chagrin, become so universal today that an appeal to God's authority—a caution so weighty even for the neo-pagan conscience and morality of Viret's time—which our Reformer makes is, for the majority of our contemporaries, clearly received as a dead letter.

---

[13] Pierre Viret, *Instruction chrétienne*, Tome I, p. 688.

CHAPTER EIGHT

A Call to Return to the Divinely-created Natural Order

In our time, the moral or civil appeal to natural order contains scarcely any meaning, for, in the view of our Modernity, the physical laws of nature have no moral or legal meaning since they retain no more than their mathematical significance. The meaning of the modern abstract laws of nature is thus reduced to their merely scientific—that is, measurable—aspect. What's more, this natural order (that of the famous *natural laws* of mathematical-experimental science) has, since the beginning of the seventeenth century, been founded on the spirit of our Modernity, the methodological exclusion of God (the final cause) and the meaning that the Word of God provides to our understanding of the world (the formal cause), thus abandoning modern science—which has become, for our culturally-respectable intelligence, an inescapable model—to merely material and efficient causality, that is, let us insist, only mechanical and utilitarian. This clearly explains the quasi-irresistible technical power of modern science, void as it now is of all ethical, legal, and teleological limits.

For Viret, as for other Reformers such as Martin Luther, Philip Melanchthon, William Tyndale, John Calvin, Heinrich Bullinger, Hugh Latimer, William Whitaker, Peter Martyr Vermigli, Girolamo Zanchi, Theodore Beza and, later, Jean Diodati, Gisbert Voetius, John Owen, Anthony Burgess, Francis Turretin, Benedict Pictet, and Johannes Althusius (to mention only the most eminent Reformers), the order of nature (natural law) remained the order of man's right conscience. The case laws produced by this right conscience are largely in conformity to biblical law, but also to the order of creation itself. For the creation, under God's covenantal perspective, also has a multifaceted meaning—both moral and political—revealed to us not only by the entire Law-Word of God, the *Tota Scriptura,* but also by every aspect of the creational order and even by our human language itself. For our divinely-given means of expression, by its very nature of naming things—the appropriate universals—according to their natures, also possesses a metaphorical, symbolic, analogical significance which often speaks to us of heavenly and divine truths in the familiar tongue of earthly realities.

This natural order (natural, creational law), found in the legal traditions of the Ancients and thus also in Thomas Aquinas whose thought is so strongly associated with the Bible, and that of Aristotle—but also (and above all) in Moses himself and throughout the entire Bible—was received by the Reformers as coming from the very hand of God (His eternal law ordaining all other laws). The task of a properly-instructed man—both philosophically and theologically—consisted in detecting the stable nature of God's creatures as revealed by their substantial sensibly-observable forms whose understanding (as abstract universals) is accessible to us through the mind. This meaning of the creatures is thus inherent to their natures, for it was given them by the Creator from the creation of all things. Because these "natures" are stable and well-ordered, man can, by attentive observation, discover within them their character and meaning (their substantial form).

When all is said and done, the meaning inherent to every creature has been given to it by God and not manufactured by the quibbling of man's autonomous reasoning, as is the case with the artificial cosmos—that manmade order of the world, the "technocosmos," as the philosopher Jan Marejko called it—constructed from start to finish by our mathematical and experimental science. The real universe—not that of our humanly-fabricated scientific and technological worldview closed in on itself—manifests an order which is that of God's creation, that is, a differentiated and hierarchical harmony that is God's cosmic handiwork. For the Modernists, on the other hand—particularly since the emergence of the philosophical subjectivism of Bacon, Descartes, and with both Galileo and Newton, the universal mathematicization of the sciences as the almost exclusive mode of accessing reality, the order of nature has become the object of the mathematical-experimental construction of scientists and technicians. The *solve et coagula* of the alchemists (so dear to Newton) was thus transposed into the *resolutive* and *compositive* method of our modern sciences. We here find ourselves confronted with the famed flying island of Laputa, situated in the clouds, that Jonathan Swift revealed in the third part of *Gulliver's Travels* in his both brilliant and prophetic satirical epic.

The modern cosmos is thus now, by means of our scientific method, arrogantly and synthetically *constructed* as an abstract (imaginary!)[1] conceptual framework by the science and technology of men who no longer humbly *receive* it from the hand of the Creator. The cosmos of the Ancients, such as it was, reflected to a large degree the created order as it had come forth from the hand of God. Every aspect of reality thus possesses its specific meaning. Both pagan as well as modern myths (Adam Smith, Karl Marx, Charles Darwin, Friedrich Nietzsche, Sigmund Freud, Carl Gustav Jung, Teilhard de Chardin) have vainly searched for the truth in an attempt to discover the meaning of both cosmic and human reality, but the Law-Word of God alone is the supreme infallible revealer of it. This creational meaning, innate to the creatures, expresses an objective natural order (inherent to the object itself), an order which is—within its inherent limited variations—fully stable, coherent, complete, and comprehensive (that is, in its created substantial form). Its identity and meaning is discoverable, in part, *naturally* by the attentive observation of human understanding (Aristotle) and, in a much more secure and complete way, *supernaturally* through the Bible.

---

[1] See Amos Funkenstein, *Theology and the Scientific Imagination from the Middle Ages to the Seventeenth Century* (Princeton University Press, Princeton, NJ, 1986).

This natural order (being itself a creation of God) is in perfect conformity with all that is spoken of it to us in the divine, written, infallible, and canonical Word of God. This biblical meaning therefore corresponds to the order of creation, an order in a concrete covenantal relationship with the Creator—the blessings and curses of the Covenant affect nature also—as well as within the various spheres of laws (as described by Herman Dooyeweerd, treading here unknowingly in the footsteps of Thomas Aquinas and Aristotle!). This is the creational order—a natural order—that we have, with the assistance of Pierre Viret, for some time begun to examine. The meaning of this creational order, which we call *nature,* is thus (in its various aspects) at the same time fully material, mathematical, biological, social, civil, political, economic, aesthetic, metaphysical, moral, spiritual, and theological, all which spheres cohere together without commingling or confusion.[2] Such an order is also reflected in every aspect of the human legal order, as much as it agrees with the purpose of law, which is always to declare "that which is just," leading us to discover a jurisprudential system carefully adapted to its specific purpose. The nature of such a judicial order is defined by the divinely-revealed standards of the Law, that is, by the various aspects of the Torah—the ultimate norm of our conscience—as they are perceived in all Scripture (*Tota Scriptura*) through the entire body of Biblical Law: moral, ceremonial, and civil.[3]

Today, apparently, the law (or *positive* law) scarcely enjoys any connection to a justice which transcends it and which would provide us with a foundation of judicial truth, both ethical and legal, revealed and moral, human and divine, earthly and heavenly and, at the same time, both transcendent and immanent. Our modern judicial science, "deprived of both faith and law," corresponds essentially to the judicial mechanisms of the prevailing systems of both subjective and arbitrary voluntarist

---

[2] See here the writings of the great South African Reformed philosopher and theologian, Hendrik Stoker.
[3] On this subject see the forthcoming title, Jean-Marc Berthoud, *In Defense of God's Law* (Zurich Publishing, Tallahassee, FL).

positive law. Such laws are decreed by the arbitrary democratic passions, fantasies, and hedonistic utopian dreams, both utilitarian and immanent—in fact purely voluntarist—of legislators and judges who play at being God (Gen. 3). These tendencies have been theoretically conceptualized by such legal theoreticians as Jeremy Bentham (1748-1832), John Austin (1790-1859), or Hans Kelsen (1881-1973). Within the context of such an iniquitous judicial framework as is today prevalent in almost all law schools, it would be perfectly absurd to think it possible for a just legal system or a normative order of justice to be founded on our modern scientific natural order. This can only be done from a natural (cosmic or creational) order of justice established on transcendent and creational biblical norms. For such a vision of a truly just legal reality is unthinkable both within the context of a purely mathematical worldview and within that of the atrophied and cauterized human conscience of our day.

In this view of the cosmos—that of our Modernity—the universe is nothing more than a nominalistic process of brute matter in constant evolution. The judicial science to which it corresponds (as is also the case with its corresponding "philosophies" and "theologies") itself lacks any kind of objective norms. For it is intrinsically and methodologically deprived of its proper and inherent legal object: that which is just and right. Thus human justice is radically separated from both its transcendent (heavenly) meaning—that which is objectively right—as well as from the immanent (earthly) order—that of a concrete justice appropriate to the human species. On the other hand, the practice of a true system of law does not in any way have as its purpose—as has our present intrinsically iniquitous legal systems—the manufacturing by arbitrary legislative fiat or judicial precedent of an unjust judicial order. A just judicial order can only acknowledge the prior existence of such true justice, publicly declaring through specific concrete legal judgments what is established by the Creator as objectively just. Our modern voluntarist system of law thus no longer gives a faithful echo to the righteous thought of the Creator and, consequently, to the practice of true justice. This "modern positive legislated" law is, consequently, because of its erroneous foundations, deprived of all justice. Such injustice imposed as law cannot in the long run be anything but consensual, relative, evolutionary, and ever-changing. It is deprived of any connection to stable Truth. In short, just like the scientific world whose structure it reflects—a world, let us repeat, *without God or Law*—our modern legal system can, by definition, only be morally and judicially meaningless and, consequently, can only be a source of evil and of civil, political, psychological, and social chaos—that is, an expression of God's judgments.

It is within this cultural context that Pierre Viret's ethical and legal thought is extraordinarily beneficial for us, gathering together as it does earthly things with heavenly, unifying into a single bundle the ancient view of law with the biblical concept of human and divine justice, the law given by God in the Bible and its expression in the truly diverse—and in their creaturely differentiation, equally just—legal codes of men. May God grant us the grace to allow this great Swiss Reformer, this colleague and friend of John Calvin and William Farel, to now speak to us (through his conversations between such captivating characters) of that just Christian view of both the Law and the Gospel ordered by God for the good of mankind.

In conclusion, listen to the wisdom, both human and heavenly, of the psalmist:

> I will hear what God the LORD will speak: for he will speak peace unto his people, and to his saints: but let them not turn again to folly. Surely his salvation is nigh them that fear him; that glory may dwell in our land. Mercy and truth are met together; righteousness and peace have kissed each other. Truth shall spring out of the earth; and righteousness shall look down from heaven. Yea, the LORD shall give that which is good; and our land shall yield her increase. Righteousness shall go before him; and shall set us in the way of his steps.
>
> Psalm 85:8-13

CHAPTER NINE[1]

Viret and the Application of God's Law to Society

Over 400 pages of the first volume of Viret's *Instruction chrétienne* (large folio pages, small print) are dedicated to a complete treatise on the detailed application of the Ten Commandments to every aspect of reality. It is the finest exposition of the Law of God that it has been my privilege to read.[2] Not only do we find in Viret's *Instruction chrétienne* a detailed application of God's Word to the practical problems of Christian living in every aspect of personal and social life, but this is done with an admirable sense of theological balance and of the delicate relation of dogmatics to ethics, together with the constant implicit purpose of favoring the preaching of the Gospel, of extending God's kingdom, and of bringing all honor and praise to the Lord Jesus Christ.

In the *Preface* Viret sets forth his central purpose with the utmost clarity: "My aim in this volume has been to produce an exposition of the Law of God, a Law which must be regarded as the rule for every other law through which men are to be directed and governed."[3] He adds, "Every science, human prudence, and all wisdom of men must be put into relation to God as a gift

---

[1] The following text is adapted from a lecture given for I Congresso Internacional, *Reforma Protestante y Libertades en Europa*, Facultad de Communicaciòn, University of Sevilla, Spain on March 31st, 2009. This talk was later adapted and published in Jean-Marc Berthoud, "Viret as Ethicist" in *Pierre Viret: a Forgotten Giant of the Reformation* (Zurich Publishing, 2010), pp. 27-48. Used with permission.
[2] See page 26, footnote 30 for publication information on the English translation of Viret's commentary on the Ten Commandments.
[3] Pierre Viret, *Instruction chrétienne en la doctrine de la Loy et de l'Évangile* (Geneva, 1564), p. 249.

which proceeds from him."⁴

Then Viret goes on to define his purpose more precisely:

> Thus God has included in this Law every aspect of that moral doctrine by which men may live well. For in these Laws he has done infinitely better than the Philosophers and all their books, whether they deal with Ethics, Economics or Politics. This Law stands far above all human legislation, whether past, present or future and is above all laws and statutes edicted by men. It follows that whatever good men may put forward has previously been included in this law, and whatever is contrary to it is of necessity evil. . . . This law, if it is rightly understood, will furnish us with true Ethics, Economics and Politics. It is incomparably superior to what we find in the teachings of Aristotle, Plato, Xenophon, Cicero and like thinkers who have taken such pains to fashion the customs of men.⁵

And Viret concludes his *Preface* with these words:

> For as it can only be God Himself who is able to give us such a perfect Law by which we are truly enabled to govern ourselves, likewise it is only He who can provide us with Princes and Magistrates, Pastors and Ministers gifted with the capacity of applying this Law. Further, He is fully able to shape such men into adequate instruments for his service and to grant them the authority necessary for the accomplishment of the duties of their office. Thus armed they are enabled by God to maintain those over whom they rule (and of whose welfare they are accountable to God) in a spirit of due subjection. For, just as He has granted us this Law in order that we might clearly know what we lack, so he likewise grants us, through Jesus Christ his Son, the Holy Ghost by whom our hearts are renewed and through whom we receive those gifts and graces so

---

⁴ Viret, *Instruction chréstienne*, p. 274.
⁵ Viret, *Instruction chréstienne*, p. 255.

necessary for the accomplishment of our vocation.[6]

Such a view of the overarching authority and supreme wisdom of God's Law led Pierre Viret to a detailed examination of the particular duties of men within the bounds of their specific vocations.

From all this it is clear that Viret's great friendship with John Calvin (his contemporary) in no way prevented him from, on occasion, expressing divergent theological views while, of course, sharing the same Reformed convictions on all fundamental points of doctrine. The Reformation thus gives us a striking example of the way basic doctrinal unity is in no way exclusive of a certain theological diversity. It is the mechanical conformism of an effeminate age which cannot stomach disagreements on secondary matters in the Church. Thus, on the question of the extent of the application of the detail of the Mosaic Law to our present situation, Viret held a significantly different position from that of Calvin. Robert Linder defines this difference in this way: "Viret, unlike Calvin, was ready to extend openly the authority of the Bible over the State."[7]

It is enlightening here to compare Viret and Calvin's exegesis of specific texts. In his *Sermons on Deuteronomy*, for example, we often find that Calvin, while not ignoring the detailed practical implications of the Mosaic Law, nonetheless pays much less attention than Viret to their immediate meaning and to their application to the political, economic, and social problems of his time. Let us briefly contrast these two different attitudes by showing how they apply to a specific Biblical text.

> Thou shalt not have in thy bag divers weights, a great and a small.
> Thou shalt not have in thy house divers measures, a great and a small.
> But thou shalt have a perfect and just weight, a perfect and just measure shalt thou have, that thy

---

[6] Viret, *Instruction chréstienne*, pp. 255-256.
[7] Linder, *The Political Ideas of Pierre Viret*, p. 63.

days may be lengthened in the land which the Lord thy God giveth thee.

For all that do such things, and all that do unrighteously, are an abomination unto the Lord thy God.

Deuteronomy 25:13-16

Let's first look at Calvin's comments on this text in his *Sermons on Deuteronomy*.

> There are two things by which above all we offend our neighbor. For some abandon themselves to fraud and evil practices, whilst others proceed by aggressions and insults. However, with regard to hidden malice, the worst means of all is that by which weights and measures are falsified. For just weights and just measures enable men to commerce with one another without dispute or harm. Without money with which to buy and to sell what confusion would ensue! Now goods are also often distributed by weight and measure. Thus when the falsification of money, weights, or measurements occur it is the social bond itself between men which is broken. Men are then reduced to the state of cats and dogs whom it is impossible to approach without fear. We must thus not be surprised if our Lord manifests such detestation for the practice of falsifying weights and measures for he shows thereby that we deal here with the worst and the most detestable kind of robbery imaginable. For when a thief proposes to carry out some thieving knavery he only attacks one man. True he will go from one victim to another. But we know that a thief cannot multiply himself to such a degree as to enable him to rob the whole world at one go. But whoever establishes false weights and false measures is not particular as to whom he will rob. He indeed robs all and sundry alike. Thus he so perverts the common order of society that the bond of humanity is broken. When no integrity or loyalty remains in those

things which should normally help men to maintain themselves in their condition, what then will become of law and justice?[8]

Calvin then goes on to apply this particular law to what he calls 'general doctrine.' By this he means the application of the principle of integrity which stands behind this specific law to divers aspects of the Christian life. He speaks of loyalty in business dealings; of just prices in commerce; of compassion for the poor; of the hypocrisy of pretending to be a Christian and neglecting these practical duties towards one's neighbor; of man's innate corruption; and of the necessity for loyalty and integrity in human relationships. He concludes on the following note:

> Let us all fear what has here been shown and may each of us walk in loyalty and integrity with regard to his neighbor. Let those engaged in commerce see that their balances and their measures be correct, that their merchandise be genuine, that they should falsify nothing and that all should use such loyalty one to another that everyone recognize that there indeed exists a law which exercises its effective rule over our hearts.[9]

Pierre Viret proceeds in a very different manner. He devotes no less than fifty-five large folio pages of small print to a detailed exposition of the Eighth Commandment.[10] On our particular text his comments cover six pages. Instead of drawing general moral lessons from the particular statute as Calvin does,

---

[8] John Calvin, Sermon CXLIV du vendredi 14 février 1556, Deutéronome 25, 13-19, *Opera Omnia, Vol. XXVIII*, p. 236. Author's translation.
[9] Calvin, Sermon CXLIV, p. 237. In the third volume of his *Harmony of the Pentateuch* (Calvin Translation Society, Edinburgh, 1854), Calvin's remarks on the Eighth Commandment take up sixty-nine pages of exegetical comments (p. 110-179). The passage in question is examined together with Leviticus 19:35-36. We find the same characteristics in his commentary as in his sermons.
[10] Pierre Viret, *Instruction Chrétienne Vol. I*, pp. 586-611. This commentary is available in English under the title Pierre Viret, *Thou Shalt Not Steal* (Psalm 78 Ministries, 2017, 126 pages).

Viret takes great pains to study the various specific applications of this precise statute in a variety of aspects of commercial dealings. That is, he develops the case law of this particular Biblical statute. He does this in such a way that, though his remarks are carefully adapted to the conditions of his time and culture, they nevertheless remain applicable today. His comments in no way constitute a distortion of the Mosaic significance of the particular law under consideration.

Let us first look at the subdivisions into which he orders his material, divisions marked by the following headings:

— Theft committed by the falsification of quantity and of weights and measures of things sold and distributed and how such theft is detestable in the sight of Holy Scripture.

— Of the invention and usage of money, of counterfeiters and of the magnitude of the crime committed by the counterfeiting of money.

— Of thieves and counterfeiters of the Word of God and of the thefts both of men's souls and of their goods committed by such means.

— Of those who clip coins and of those who consciously use false money and particularly of those responsible for the public treasury.

— Of corruption by bribes and of merchants who buy and sell justice and of the effect of this on the poor.

— Of thefts committed in the sale of foodstuffs by their falsification and the dangers which such corruptions produce.

— Of the attention magistrates should give to the quality of foodstuffs.

— Of the danger of falsification of medicines by doctors and druggists.

— Of the importance of the law given by God on weights and measures and of his threats against those who falsify them.

Speaking of the falsification of weights and measures, Viret writes:

This theft is also very frequent and quite common because it is much easier to steal from men by this means than to alter the substance and materials or to corrupt them, because it is much easier to perceive the deception in such an alteration or corruption than it is in this matter of weights and measures. For, when we buy or sell, we must for the most part trust the weights and measures of the merchants with whom we deal. For we cannot always carry our own weights and measures with us. . . . Because of this, the iniquity of those who falsify it is so much greater because they so wickedly deceive those who trust in them. By this they are like public thieves and highway robbers.[11]

Viret aptly applies this statute to counterfeiters as in ancient times the inequality of the weight of coins made it necessary to weigh them in order to measure their exact worth.

Firstly, counterfeiters are very dangerous and harmful. This is because money and the type of money (gold, silver, and other metals) has been employed by men to more easily conduct business and to have the easiest means of sharing with one another the goods which God has given them. For the course of commercial dealings is nothing more than an exchange made between men by which some give to others something they possess, and accept something else in payment, according to the value of the goods exchanged. Now, because it is very difficult to transport the things which we have for trade, money is used instead of them, according to the price they are valued at, which is truly much easier to carry and much more fitting than anything else for all kinds of trade and merchandise.

Therefore, seeing that God has given this means to man so that they can assist each other more easily, those who pervert and confound this order are a grave scourge to the public good and to all human

---
[11] Pierre Viret, *Thou Shalt Not Steal* (Psalm 78 Ministries, 2017), p. 48.

society. Thus they are worthy of grievous punishment, and this even more so because they create such terrible confusion among men. For men cannot live without trading with each other. Therefore whoever removes this means is like a public criminal who slits the throat of the entire community of mankind, for by his fraud he destroys the trust and honesty without which human society can neither exist nor be preserved. For, if trust and honesty are removed, no one can be sure of anything. Therefore by this men live in terrible trouble and in a disorder the like of which has never been surpassed.[12]

Today the counterfeiting of money has become the specialty of our Central Banks who outrageously rob the community by their fractional reserve banking and their creation of *fiat* ('virtual') money out of thin air. The result of such monetary creation is, of course, the uncontrolled expansion of every kind of public and private debt, the destruction of the productivity of society by the concentration of such capital in speculative transactions, and the development of our modern boom–bust cycle of inflation and monetary restriction and the widespread expansion of totally unproductive speculation. Viret would have had much to say from a biblical perspective on our present monetary system. He was fully aware of these problems as they manifested themselves in his own time. He goes on to write acidly of the sin of the State counterfeiting the means of exchange in the following sparkling dialogue:

> TIMOTHY: It seems to me that we could rightly add to the counterfeiters all those who clip coins and who diminish their weight, and who use false and unjust weights knowingly, and not by ignorance, as often happens. For, though these work differently than those called counterfeiters, yet, seeing that their deeds tend nearly to the same end as the others, they all end up at the same place even though the means are some-

---

[12] Viret, *Thou Shalt Not Steal*, p. 50.

what different.

DANIEL: You touch upon a matter in which the hands of those who have the management of public moneys are often as stained as the others. When they receive money, they are meticulous in checking to be sure that each coin has its full weight and value and that nothing is debased, and that nothing is missing and the money has not been miscounted. But, when it comes time to disburse and pay the salaries of those who have served either in the church or for the public good, or to give something to the poor, God knows with what loyalty and faithfulness they do their job.

TIMOTHY: I have known some who would (as I think) make a great conscience of never making a full payment to those whom they dealt with, and particularly to the poor, without always retaining some portion either of the wages that were due them or of the charity which was commanded them, and they do this either by using counterfeit money or unjust weights, or spurious bills. They also think that the poor ought not to complain, even though they are so openly robbed and cheated.

DANIEL: These are not only thieves and counterfeiters, but are also swindlers and public menaces, worse than those who rob a man in the woods. For what worse could they do besides taking away their very life?

TIMOTHY: Yet they never receive what is owed them from those who make them payments without counting it properly or weighing and testing it, not in the sort that they give to others who do not have the boldness to resist their tyranny and theft.

DANIEL: You can be assured of this.[13]

---

[13] Viret, *Thou Shalt Not Steal*, pp. 52-53.

But Viret does not hesitate to also apply this very practical commandment to spiritual matters. Let us quote a last passage from his dialogues on the Ten Commandments.

> TIMOTHY: If these are so dangerous and are punished so grievously, what can we say of those who counterfeit the Word of God, which is the true spiritual stamp and currency of His people for the preservation of the Church and spiritual life?
>
> DANIEL: It is easy to judge this. Jeremiah calls the false prophets "thieves of the Word of God" because they stole the Word from the people of God by falsifying it like forgers and by setting forth their dreams and inventions instead of it. . . .
>   Not only can we truly call these men thieves of all sorts, but also murderers of souls.
>   Firstly, they are kidnappers because they entice and steal men's hearts by their false doctrine, and steal them from God by this means. They also murder their souls because they cause them to be deprived of eternal life.
>   Secondly, they steal their eternal inheritance as well as their earthly goods, which are the main reasons why they do this.
>
> TIMOTHY: Yet there are many such thieves and falsifiers upon the earth.
>
> DANIEL: At least the entire kingdom of the Roman antichrist is well supplied with them, inasmuch as it has no other prophets than such thieves and counterfeiters who have wholly overturned and falsified the teaching of the Lord and perverted the sacraments ordained by Him.
>
> TIMOTHY: I agree with you. But how I wish that such men were not also found among those who boast themselves of the purity of the Gospel! For it is not

enough to preach without mixing in false doctrine, but it is also required to preach the Word in its entirety, without concealing anything out of fear of men or in an effort to please them.[14]

What an extraordinarily premonitory attack we have here on those liberal and modernist exegetes (falsifiers, robbers, and thieves of the Word of God) who, from Benedict Spinoza and Richard Simon at the end of the seventeenth century, led the Enlightenment war on the trustworthiness and inspired unity of the text of the Old and New Testaments.

Viret, while never minimizing the doctrinal and moral aspect of his text, pays far more attention to the immediate literal meaning of the specific law under consideration and to its detailed and very particular application to the problems of his own time and culture than do either Calvin or Bullinger. This may in part explain the fascination his preaching exercised even on those who were foreign to the faith and the great power and effectiveness of his proclamation of the Gospel.

But, in spite of these different and complementary orientations, we do not find the slightest indication of personal or theological tension in the friendship that united these great Christian leaders in their common vocation to further the Kingdom of God. In this they have much to teach us latter-day Calvinists who are all too often inclined to give way to that sectarian spirit which so banefully characterized the Corinthian Church. It is useful to hear Calvin's witness on this question in the dedication of his commentary on Titus which he addressed to his good friends Pierre Viret and William Farel:

> It will at least be a testimony to this present age and perhaps to posterity of the holy bond of friendship that unites us. I think there has never been in ordinary life a circle of friends so heartily bound to each other as we have been in our ministry. With both of you I discharged here the office of pastor, and so far from

---
[14] Viret, *Thou Shalt Not Steal,* pp. 51-52.

there being any appearance of rivalry, I always seemed to be of one mind with you. Later we were separated and you, Farel, were called to the church of Neuchâtel which you had rescued from papal tyranny and brought to Christ, and you, Viret, stand in the same relationship to the church of Lausanne.

But while each of us keeps to his own post, our union brings together God's children in Christ's fold and unites them in His body, and at the same time it scatters not only our external enemies who carry on open war against us, but those nearer internal enemies who attack us from within. This also I count among the benefits of our union, that unclean dogs whose bites cannot succeed in tearing and rending the Church only stir it up to no effect by their barking. We cannot hold their influence in too great scorn, since we have good reason to glory before God and have the clearest evidence to show to men that our alliance and friendship have been entirely consecrated to Christ's name, have hitherto been profitable to His Church, and have no other aim than that all men should be at one with Him. Farewell most excellent and honorable brethren. May the Lord Jesus continue to bless your godly labors.[15]

---

[15] David W. Torrance and Thomas F. Torrance, *Calvin's New Testament Commentaries, Vol. 10* (Eerdmans, Grand Rapids, 1980), pp. 347-348.

APPENDIX ONE

Pierre Viret, Herald of Conceptual Realism in Science: the Physical, Biological, Theological, and Moral Science of a Universe Created, Ordered, and Sustained by God

A review of Pierre Viret's *Instruction chrétienne en la Loi et l'Évangile,* Volume Three (introduced, edited, and annotated by Arthur-Louis Hofer, L'Age d'Homme, Lausanne, 2013, 928 pages).

After an initial volume dedicated to painting the portrait of the Christian Faith through a series of catechisms of increasing size and fullness,[1] a tome which ends with a description of the war that men wage against their own salvation; then, with a second volume describing the Christian worldview through one of the greatest, delightful, and most complete expositions of the Ten Commandments known to the history of the Church, we now come to the third volume of this *Instruction chrétienne en la Loi et l'Évangile,* the indisputable masterpiece of this Swiss Reformer from Lausanne, this admirable writer and theologian of such magnificent fullness who is Pierre Viret.

In this third volume we encounter the first part (which will be completed in the fourth book) of a comprehensive

---

[1] Portions of this volume have been translated into English and published under the titles: Pierre Viret, *A Simple Exposition of the Christian Faith* (Zurich Publishing, 2017) and *The Catechism of Pierre Viret* (Zurich Publishing, 2017).

commentary on the Apostles Creed.² This tome is almost entirely dedicated to an examination of the knowledge of God both through Holy Scripture, His special revelation, and His general revelation, the latter contained in the book of creation through which (as our author so clearly shows us) God also unveils His nature and attributes.

This theme takes on an extraordinary fullness when in his delightful dialogues Pierre Viret begins to address the way in which the natural world, the universe created by God, reveals the most extraordinary of natural theologies to the person truly desiring to perceive it other than through the theoretical lenses of a science which seeks to be "modern." This theology speaks to us of the created world illuminated by the written Word of God, the living Word which, at the beginning, brought the universe into being.

For, according to Viret, we must not consider the material works of God—His work of creating and ordering the universe as well as the providence by which He upholds and directs all things—solely through the revelation that these works give us of the power and order existing within God. It would be a similar narrow focus, one which focused entirely on the material power and efficacy of the world (the material and efficient causes)—and, consequently, on the exclusive attention brought to these specific attributes of its Author—which would henceforth lead the direction of the mathematical experimental sciences of nature. Such thinking would, several decades after the death of our theologian, surrender the study of the cosmos of God to the sole language of mathematical precision, utility, and practicability.

All divine work must, according to Viret, be perceived in the spirit of the parables, symbols, and images issuing from the created order, in a way of understanding the world which penetrates every part in the familiar, concrete, and colorful

---

² Portions of Pierre Viret's commentary on the Apostles Creed have been translated into English and published under the titles *Marvelous Trinity: the Believer's Hope and Delight*; *Jesus Christ: the Believer's Comfort and Joy*; and *His Glorious Bride: A Practical Look at Jesus Christ's Church* (Psalm 78 Ministries, 2019).

tongue of the Holy Scriptures. It is truly this proverbial ordinary language of men that Aesop in his fables reflected as well as, much later, that of his imitator, the last fabler of our Europe, Jean de la Fontaine. Thus, in the sixteenth century, at the end of Christendom, Pierre Viret turns from the abstractions of burgeoning modernity to recover the wisdom of the bestiaries and moral studies of animal life of ancient and medieval science. Everything in nature contains meaning, for (as Viret shows us) even in its smallest details creation reveals the reflection of its Creator in this fullness of meaning and wisdom that He Himself bestowed on it. Like Aristotle, Viret doesn't cease to meditate on the natural order; like Plato, he always sees within it the testimony of a reality which surpasses nature; but, by his submission to Scripture, he also discovers a spiritual, theological, and moral meaning written within it that ancient paganism scarcely glimpsed from afar.

Viret's masterful work is truly a biblical response suitable to satisfy the thirst which haunts us for an understanding of the world other than what issues from the desert of the purely measurable or quantifiable sciences and from that of a pantheistic jungle which turns a formless and savage nature into idolatry. This third volume of *Instruction chrétienne en la Loi et l'Évangile* truly arrives at its proper time, fulfilling the expectation of those who seek to perceive in the good and blessed creation of God, enlightened by the light of His written revelation, the fullness of meaning and beauty which, by our insane fury of abstraction, we have deprived ourselves of for almost five centuries.

Let us thank the Association Pierre Viret, *Editions l'Age d'Homme,* and pastor Arthur-Louis Hofer (without whose wise and often colorful labor these three volumes would never have seen the light of day) for once more granting us access to this immense work which, in such an understandable and captivating manner, opens anew for us the gates to the theological, spiritual, and moral concrete meaning of divine creation, a work conceived by Pierre Viret at the very moment of the suppression of this immemorial creational vision, that of such a true and so vivifying a vision of the world. Some considered its demise final under the weight of the bewildering confusion issuing from the apparently irresistible abstractions of a new worldview, a vision from which God, meaning, and beauty would be entirely excluded.

Jean-Marc Berthoud
Lausanne
January 21, 2014

APPENDIX TWO

The True Issue of the Debate Between Science and Faith

I include an excerpt from a discussion with a scientist friend, a text which, it seems to me, sets forth the true issues of our discussion.

Our debate over creation approaches the question from the wrong direction, that of specific questions. Within the framework of prevailing contemporary thought, these details of the biblical account of creation have become incomprehensible, absurd, and inadmissible to the mentality of our contemporaries, whether scientists or not. We're taken up with details when we should be focusing on the big picture, the conflict of paradigms, of incompatible, mutually-exclusive, irreconcilable worldviews.

We live today—this assertion unfortunately applies to the entire world at present—under the domination of a mathematical, utilitarian, and amoral (that is, unspiritual) vision of the world, of a universe where (as the pagan Aristotle would have put it) the final and formal cause—God and the comprehensive meaning of all reality which is His revealed Word—are methodologically excluded. Such an exclusion concerns the qualitative, moral, and spiritual domains belonging to the very nature of the cosmos itself. This meaning has been uprooted from our vision of the universe (the system of the universe constructed by modern science) and from our present worldview, as it has been manufactured and consolidated by us in the course the past four centuries, and which has led us today to a total impasse.

Let me give an example. Water can truly be chemically

defined by the formula H_2O, which describes the atomic composition of the molecule water which we observe in three quite distinct forms: liquid, solid, and gas. But water, as a natural phenomenon, contains within itself other meanings just as objective, just as significant, more varied meanings which we must not bypass simply because they are non-mathematical and relegate them to the subjective—that is, irrelevant—metaphorical, imaginary, spiritual, and symbolic realm.

Water has the ability to give life to the body; this biological characteristic can then relate to that divine water which gives us eternal life; water cleanses the body, this meaning can also relate to the action of the Holy Spirit who purifies our souls.

You see, the universal pretensions of the scientific revolution dating from the beginning of the seventeenth century have managed to destroy the unity of human thought. This is exactly what the Anglo-American poet T. S. Eliot perceived at the beginning of the twentieth century in evoking the tragedy of the disastrous split between understanding and sensibility. That is, between a quantitative science (that which can be measured) which alone is deemed true, and that of a qualitative science (one which cannot be measured quantitatively). This latter was handed over to the external darkness of a superstitious knowledge, as forbidding as it was obsolete. On one hand was the formula H_2O as truth, on the other everything else was abandoned to insignificance. The two opposing worlds—science and culture—scarcely know how to communicate with one another. We are thus handed over, bound hand and foot by our educational and academic training, to a dualist, Gnostic, and schizophrenic world from which all metaphysical, theological, and biblical meaning is irreparably banished.

In such a world (the system of the modern world itself), it is clear that the creation account has scarcely any meaning at all. It can no longer be assimilated by our "instructed" contemporaries—that is, formatted in a utilitarian manner—without undergoing serious reductions and modifications. In particular, within this new universe (our scientific model), all must be measurable or quantifiable to possess a right to meaning.

This is the reign of the famed disassociation between *sense* (reduced to a solely mathematical meaning) and *sensibility* (reduced solely to an emotional, metaphorical, symbolic, spiritual, and non-conceptualist meaning).

The modern quantitative world, oriented solely in this mathematical sense, is in no way able to assimilate a qualitative view of the world, which was that of the old world before the scientific revolution. This former view of the world was still able to include within its cosmology the mathematical sphere itself, but it refused to consider the measurable as the sole model of all reality.

The beliefs of Bacon, Descartes, and Galileo determined that their material worldview necessarily excluded final and formal causes, those of Aristotle, the Bible, and the entire creation. The same can be said for the apotheosis of this worldview *fossilized* as it was in Newton's mathematical system: according to him, science (*sense*) is placed on one side and alchemy—his hobby— (*sensibility*), on the other.

When Cardinal Bellarmine criticized Galileo for imagining the material world in the light of mathematics alone to the exclusion of the creative Word itself, Galileo responded by affirming that "Within the universe of physics, mathematics are superior to the Bible." The Bible at the outset was excluded from his scientific system, which alone was worthy of enlightened understanding.

Laplace, when asked by Napoleon, "Monsieur Laplace, where does God fit into your system?", replied, "Sire, I have no need of such a hypothesis!" God, relegated to the status of a hypothesis, was excluded from his system from the outset.

What is excluded from the start can never be found at the finish. Thus a single model is installed in people's minds in such an insidious way as to inhabit the intelligence of the inhabitants of the entire globe. This unitary model, that of an exclusively quantified science, is today both omnipresent and has become the sole—universally accepted—normative reality. From such a positivistic, utilitarian, and rationalist *scientistic system,* God, the normative teaching of the Bible, and the understanding we draw from our *intelligent sensibility*—so rich and so varied a method of knowledge (that of things that can be observed directly by the senses)—are strictly excluded!

God and the meaning that He gives to all things by the divine Word—a meaning written both within the Bible and within the very order of the creatures—are thus banished from our world. This divine Word which gives meaning to all creatures visible and invisible disappears from the cultural horizon of a civilization that is inherently and intrinsically without God—that is, atheist.

It is by turning to the mind of God, that of the Bible, received by a simple act of faith, similar to—as Christ tells us—that of a little child, that we can be freed from the yoke of such a deadly bondage by the redemptive work of Jesus Christ, in order that we might access the life of God, both present and eternal.

Made in the USA
Monee, IL
10 April 2022